The Hidden Country

THE HIDDEN COUNTRY about which the author writes is that fascinating world of living things all around us. Often unseen or unnoticed, either because they are so common or so inconspicuous, we are rarely aware of their absorbing variety, complexity and adaptability. It is a world of nature which can be experienced at first hand within minutes and yards from home.

Many of the common insects, grasses, lichens and plants seldom discussed in nature books are described here in detail. Emphasis has been laid throughout on the value of personal observation, with many suggestions for experiments and other practical work.

Imbuing the text with his own enthusiasm and deep involvement in the material he writes about, the author has prepared precise and delicate pen and ink drawings illustrating many of the extraordinary life forms he describes.

The Hidden Country
Nature on your doorstep

JOHN RICHARDS

Illustrated by the author

S. G. Phillips ⚡ *New York*

Library of Congress Cataloging in Publication Data

Richards, John, 1926-
    The hidden country.

    SUMMARY: Describes the characteristics of many
commonly-found insects and plants.
    1. Natural history—Juvenile literature.
[1. Natural history] I. Title.
QH48.R5   1973   500.9   72-12745
ISBN: 0-87599-195-5

To my daughter
Gillian

Acknowledgements

The author wishes to thank the Editor of *The Countryman* for permission to quote the verse by C.H.P. on page 18. He is also grateful for permission to use Figures 3 to 6, and much of Chapter 3, which originally formed part of an article which he wrote for that magazine.

George Allen & Unwin Ltd. have kindly permitted use of the quotation from Maurice Maeterlinck's *The Life of the Ant*, which appears on page 22.

The author is also grateful for the considerable help provided by his wife in the preparation of *The Hidden Country*.

He is no true naturalist who fails
to perceive beauty in even the most
despised creatures.

EDWARD H. ROBERTSON
1868

Contents

Illustrations

11

1 · *The Country in the Town*

Unless you were interested in Nature, you would not have picked up this book in the first place, but if you live in a town, you probably don't have the opportunity to get out into the country as often as you would like. It would be a big mistake to think that the country is the only place where you can be a practical amateur naturalist, as I hope to show you.

If you want to see wild life which is strange and interesting, even within highly developed areas, all you need to do is look. Much of the secret is merely to look rather more closely than you might need to do in the open country; in addition, you should examine, not just the obviously unusual things which you may find, but also the things which are most common, and most familiar.

It is largely a matter of mental attitude and approach: once you start to think of grass as a varied and beautiful flowering plant, of the garden slug as a hunting animal, of the ladybird as a voracious predator, and of the horsetails and mosses as miniature descendants of the coal forests, things around you look quite different. There is nearly as much beauty and drama and cause for surprise and interest

13

in a few square feet of garden as in an acre of remote wood-
land, if you know how to find it.

The back garden is quite a profitable hunting ground, if
you have one, especially if a bit of it is shady and neglected.
Public parks, in particular the less laid-out variety, are also
good. Perhaps the best of all is the plot of waste ground,
the building site which is awaiting development, or the odd
bank or hedge or overgrown corner which it seems to be
the responsibility of no one to keep tidy.

You will find little mention in this book of the birds, the
butterflies and moths, and the bees which come into our
towns and gardens. This in no way suggests that I do not
consider them of very great interest, but comes about
largely because so many books describe and discuss these
far better than I could ever hope to do. In addition, most
people are consciously *aware* of these creatures: my concern
has been primarily with the neglected, the overlooked, and
the inconspicuous.

The hidden country is, then, within easy reach of most
people, wherever they live. If you cannot find all the things
I have described within a mile of your home, you will
certainly be able to find most of them. What is perhaps
more important is that the very act of looking will reveal
so much more wild life which is equally fascinating, and
which you probably did not know was there. This book
is an aperitif, and not a meal.

Apart from accessibility, another big advantage of the
life of the hidden country is that you can, in most cases,
take your time in studying it. You do not often have to
seize the moment when something occurs, and make the
most of it. Usually, you can watch as often and for as long

as you like. Even the action, and the drama, can frequently be reproduced, almost at will.

In some cases you can, without damage or loss, take home the object of your interest for closer study, which is rarely possible or even desirable with the larger creatures of the country. Sometimes you can even set up a sufficiently natural environment in a fish bowl or something similar, to keep some of them for a while. This is a considerable help, and you will find that the results are usually well worth the effort expended.

If you merely want to read, without doing any observation yourself, there is no harm in that. This is in no way a textbook or a guide to identification: it is intended only as an introduction to some of the creatures and plants which are all around you. If in any way I succeed in making you start looking for yourself, so much the better, for you will get much more pleasure in the long run from your own observations.

For those of you who do wish to explore the hidden country yourselves, a magnifying glass of some kind is, if not essential, extremely useful. Almost any kind is better than none, but the small folding pocket variety, which gives about ten times magnification, is very suitable. It is easy to carry, not likely to be damaged readily, and quite powerful enough for most purposes.

I would strongly recommend that you try to draw what you see. It does not matter whether you are a good or a poor artist for this job, but I think that you will probably be agreeably surprised at your success. The object of the drawing is not primarily to produce an interesting picture, but to increase the amount of detail which you notice. You will not be able to draw a ladybird or a snail or a grass flower without repeated and careful observation, and you will soon find that it is the detailed observation which reveals the most interesting facets, rather than the rapid overall look.

Here, then, is a glimpse of the hidden country.

2 · God's Little Thief and the Ant Cows

A garden, an allotment, a scrap of waste ground—any-where, in fact, where wild creatures can find a living—is a battleground. As in any bit of open country, there are the hunters and the hunted, the meat eaters and the vegetarians who provide the meat. The hunters vary in size, and appetite, and some are both hunters and hunted at the same time.

The hunters which come most readily to mind are the spiders, with flies of various kinds as their principal prey. But there are many others, and all we can do here is to dip into the bag and make a very small selection. Let us look first of all at some of the victims, choosing ones for whom we have no great love, anyway.

The aphids—the greenfly and plant lice—must be well known to anyone who has a garden, however small. Even a window-box can usually produce some fine specimens. The aphids are, to say the least, a nuisance in a garden, living as they do by sucking the plant juices, and choosing the youngest and tenderest shoots. At worst, they can be a serious pest, weakening and ruining plants of many kinds on a tremendous scale.

The gardener's attitude to aphids in general is an uncompromising one, summed up by 'C.H.P.' in *The Countryman*:

Weep not for little greenflies who are orphaned in the morning;
They need no mother's tender care—by evening they'll be
*   spawning.*
Nor doth the greenfly malice bear for swatting her relations!
She just lays eggs upon the dregs of slaughtered generations.
And if she comes up smiling when with soap-suds she's been
*   plastered,*
*   There's only one thing to be done,*
*   So let me go and get my gun,*
*   And shoot the little dastard!*

In spite of their well-deserved unpopularity, the aphids are interesting creatures. They exist, for example, in winged and wingless forms, and both kinds can sometimes be found together on the same plant. Although the life cycles of aphids vary somewhat from one species to another, we can take the following sequence as being reasonably typical.

In the autumn, mating occurs, and the eggs are laid in a protected position. When the spring comes, these eggs hatch out into wingless females only. No males. The absence of males is, strangely enough, of no disadvantage at this time, because this batch of females can lay eggs which will hatch without any fertilization by a male—a process known as parthenogenesis, or virgin birth. Not only is this reproduction parthenogenetic, but, unlike the usual run of insect reproduction, it is viviparous, that is to say, the young are born alive and not hatched from eggs.

Most of the young produced this time are like their mothers—females and wingless. There may be a few males, and a few of the females may be winged, so that these can fly away to spread the race to other plants. But the males are still not necessary, and parthenogenesis goes on, perhaps for seven or eight generations in a good summer.

When the autumn comes, a change occurs, although the cause is uncertain. The succession of virgin births comes to an end with the final brood, which this time consists of sexual males and females. Fertilization and egg-laying take place, the adults die, and the eggs lie dormant throughout the winter, ready to begin a new cycle when the spring arrives.

But one of the most interesting features of the aphids is still to be mentioned. These creatures exude a sweet sticky substance from the extreme end of the abdomen, which is greatly loved by ants. Aphids are not unique in doing this, because it is a function shared by certain scale-insects and blue butterfly caterpillars.

Now, the ants do not merely like this secretion of the aphids when they come across it; many of them will go to considerable lengths to obtain it, and in some cases it forms their sole food.

Ants treat aphids very much as we treat cows, so that they are sometimes in fact referred to as 'ant cows'. Some kinds of ant seek out colonies of aphids on the plants, herd them together, and do their best to protect them from enemies. The wingless aphids have little choice but to allow themselves to be herded in this way, for the ants are considerably stronger, and are certainly much more determined. In general, however, the aphids do not seem to mind any of the ants' attentions, which in the long run are for their benefit.

Certain kinds of ant are not content merely to act as shepherds—or rather, cowherds—to the aphids. They will fence them in and construct shelters for them. Yet again, other species take aphids down into their nests for protection during the winter, through which they could certainly never survive on the surface. In the spring—in March or April—the ants can be seen carrying these aphids up from their underground home, and putting them out to pasture on plants of a suitable kind. Some will even collect the eggs of the aphids, look after them until they hatch, and rear the young, like true farmers.

Even this is not as far as the relationship between ants and aphids will go. During the course of evolution, some kinds of aphids which live on plant roots have come to be dependent on the protection of the ants, and these kinds are found only in ants' nests, living their lives below ground with their herdsmen.

As with other kinds of aphids, winged forms are sometimes hatched, only this time they are deep underground. The ants seem to appreciate what must be done when this occurs, and they will open up a path for the flying insects to emerge from the nest.

So much, then, for the ways in which ants look after their aphid 'cattle'. But how do they obtain from them the sweet sticky secretion which they so much prize? It is not stretching the analogy with cows too far to say that the ants frequently get this secretion by 'milking' the aphids.

You will see from the drawing of an aphis that it has two horns or tubes projecting upwards towards the rear end of its body. If you look at some of the older books, you may find it stated that these are the tubes from which the sweet material is obtained. This is not true, and the 'honey' is actually exuded from the extreme end of the body.

The tubes serve an entirely different function. They contain a thicker, much stickier material, which the aphis can eject to protect itself from attackers. I shall refer to these again later in this chapter.

Sometimes we can find the honey as tiny droplets on leaves where aphids are feeding, and then it is known as honey dew. Ants are quite able and ready to lick the sweet secretion off the leaves, if it is exuded in their absence, and a few species obtain it only in this way. However, many ants actually go through a process which is rather like milking, in order to cause the aphids to produce the liquid. This 'milking' consists in stroking the aphids with their antennae in a particular way, which rapidly has the desired effect. The action used is a curious mixture of stroking, caressing and tapping, which, as Charles Darwin found, is not easy to copy successfully.

Darwin tackled this problem with the patience and curiosity which was so characteristic of him, and reported the results of his experiment with equally characteristic enthusiasm. In *The Origin of Species*, he wrote:

'I removed all the ants from a group of about a dozen aphides on a dock-plant, and prevented their attendance during several hours. After this interval, I felt sure that the aphides would want to excrete. I watched them for some time through a lens, but not one excreted; I then tickled and stroked them with a hair in the same manner, as well as I could, as the ants do with their antennae; but not one excreted. Afterwards I allowed an ant to visit them, and it immediately seemed, by its eager way of running about, to be well aware what a rich flock it had discovered; it then began to play with its antennae on the abdomen first of one aphis and then of another; and each, as soon as it felt the antennae, immediately lifted up its abdomen and excreted a limpid drop of sweet juice, which was eagerly devoured by the ant. Even the quite young aphides behaved in this manner, showing that the action was instinctive, and not the result of experience. It is certain, from the observations of Huber, that the aphides show no dislike to the ants: if the latter be not present they are at last compelled to eject their excretion. But as the excretion is extremely viscid, it is no doubt a convenience to the aphides to have it removed; therefore probably they do not excrete solely for the good of the ants. Although there is no evidence that any animal performs an action for the exclusive good of another species, yet each tries to take advantage of the weaker bodily structure of other species.'

We do not know when this relationship between ants and aphids began. However, we do know that it was happening a very long time ago, certainly by the middle of the Miocene period, which makes it at least fifteen million years old. Resin oozing from trees at that time trapped and engulfed many insects; the resin solidified and became fossilized into amber, containing the insects perfectly preserved. Baltic and Sicilian amber of this period has been found containing ants, and some of them have their aphids with them.

The discovery of honey dew by the first ant to do so is wonderfully imagined and described by Maurice Maeterlinck in his book *The Life of the Ant*. I quote:

'It is highly probable that, as so often happens in our own

life, the discovery arose one day from a fortuitous circum-
stance. Roving at hazard in search of the daily ration of
honey, an ant came upon a tribe of plant-lice assembled on
the tip of a tender green shoot. A pleasant saccharine odour
reached her antennae, while her little legs were agreeably
enmeshed in a sort of delicious dew. The discovery was
miraculous, and seemed to be inexhaustible. Immediately
she proceeded to fill to bursting point her collective pouch,
her omnibus stomach, her municipal flagon, and hurried
back to the nest, where amidst the exultations and con-
vulsions of the ritual regurgitation, the magnificent find
was echoed abroad, the discovery that promised an era of
inexhaustible abundance and bliss. After an excited antennal
dialogue the whole community set out, in long files, for
the miraculous wells of plenty. A new age had commenced;
they felt they were no longer alone in a world in which all
things were unfriendly.'

Although aphids have friends and protectors in the ants,
they also have many enemies, apart from Man. This is just
as well, for if it were not so, the whole Earth would be
devastated by them in a very few seasons.

One of these enemies is the ladybird. This little beetle is
well known to everyone, not only in this country, but in
one form or another all over the world. In the United
States there are about 150 species of ladybird, with varying
numbers of spots. The most common is the nine-spotted.
Biologists use Latin names to identify plants, animals and
insects, the first word giving the *genus* (or a kind of family)
to which it belongs, and the second part giving the *species*.
With ladybirds, the part of the name which gives the
species is intended to indicate the number of spots; for

example, *septempunctata* comes from the Latin *septem* meaning seven, and *punctum*, meaning a point or spot. Even within one species, the markings can vary considerably, and the Latin names, like *Adalia bipunctata* (two-spotted), *Coccinella septempunctata* (seven-spotted), and *Adalia decempunctata* (ten-spotted), are not by any means an infallible guide to the number of spots that individuals will have. In the world as a whole, there are something like three thousand four hundred species of ladybird.

Ladybirds are true beetles, and their life cycle goes through the typical stages for such insects, that is the egg, the larva, the pupa and the imago. In the case of the ladybird the eggs are generally laid on the leaves of plants, and are yellowish in colour. These hatch out into larvae, which, like many larvae of other insects, bear no resemblance whatever to the perfect insects which they will eventually become.

The ladybird larvae are six-legged creatures, a little like earwigs in general shape, but without the forceps at the tail end which the earwig possesses. However, whereas the earwig's body is smooth, that of the ladybird larva is not. In some kinds, it is prickly; the larva of the so-called seven-spot ladybird, which is the one you are perhaps most likely to find on rose bushes, has an abdomen of unmistakable pattern, very much like crocodile skin.

In turn, the larva changes again, this time into the pupa, which corresponds with the chrysalis stage of butterflies and moths. At this period in its life, it remains anchored to the leaf by its tail, and has already attained something like the shape which it will have as a ladybird.

Finally, the skin of the pupa splits, and the adult ladybird emerges: perfect in size and shape, but still soft and pale, with few, if any, markings. A few hours in the sun is all that is needed, and the ladybird is as we all know it.

At this moment, we are not concerned particularly with the egg and pupa stages of the ladybird. We are very much concerned, however, with the imago, or perfect beetle, and with the larva, for these are both insatiable hunters. The prey—as you will by now have guessed, if you did not know before—are the aphids, the scale insects and similar plant pests.

It is partly because of the ladybird's attractive appearance and partly because of its appetite for greenfly that it is regarded kindly by most people. All over the world the ladybird is liked, as the many names by which it is called indicate: ladybug, ladycow, God's lamb, Sun-calf, God's Little Thief, and so on.

Just how good is the ladybird at dealing with aphids in a garden? Well, in the case of the crocodile-like larva, the answer is that this eats aphids incessantly. It is driven by a seemingly insatiable hunger, right from the moment it hatches from the egg. As soon as it is out, it starts to look for food, and must find it in a very short time or it is doomed.

Now, the ladybird eggs may well have been laid some distance from an aphid colony, and the larva, having no wings, may not be able to come upon a herd rapidly enough. The solution to this problem of survival for the larva is a simple one, and like so many simple solutions, it is extremely effective. The answer is cannibalism.

Immediately the larvae hatch, they look for food. If no other food is available right away, they eat one of the unhatched eggs of their own kind. Fortified for the journey, they can then set out to hunt with a greatly increased chance of survival.

It has been estimated that probably about 10 per cent of the ladybird eggs are destroyed in this way. However, this sacrifice of one out of ten is well worth it for the race as a whole, because it helps considerably to ensure that at least some of the larvae will live.

FIG. 1. The Hunter . . . (Ladybird)

The adult ladybirds are also voracious in their appetite for aphids. The one which I have drawn here was caught and placed in a tube with a rose leaf bearing thirteen aphids. In the course of roughly fifteen or twenty minutes, a dozen of these were seized and devoured.

Having located an aphis, the ladybird walked within about a quarter of an inch of it and then pounced, grasping the insect by whatever part of its body was most convenient. There seemed to be no preferred angle of attack.

Then followed a steady munching until there was nothing left—quite a different method of feeding from that of the aphis-lion, which is the larva of the lacewing fly, and which merely sucks out the juice until the aphis is an empty shell.

This particular ladybird, then, ate twelve of the thirteen aphids in the tube without hesitation, or pause for rest. The thirteenth, as the superstitious would expect, proved to be

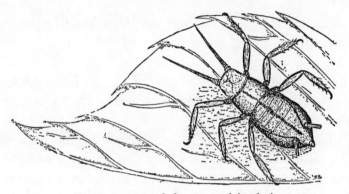

FIG. 2. . . . and the Hunted (Aphis)

a different matter. This was a big chap, compared with the others, and the ladybird seemed a little hesitant about going in to the attack. As a larva, it would not have wasted a moment before dealing effectively with number thirteen, but as an adult ladybird with twelve substantial aphids inside it already, it showed caution.

The aphis was clearly keenly aware of the danger, and obviously preferred flight to battle. But this was not possible, and the ladybird made one or two tentative lunges at it, without any result. The last time, however, it came close to the side of the aphis, which suddenly directed one of the two tubes on its abdomen towards the ladybird.

It caught the beetle across the front of its head with the sticky, viscous liquid, which, for the time being, ended the fight. The ladybird retired without further attacks, and could be seen engaged for some minutes in a vigorous cleaning-up procedure. I did not see the end of the incident, but the course which it followed is not hard to deduce. Some time later, the aphis had disappeared, while the ladybird had not.

Ladybirds, because of their usefulness in dealing with insect pests, were used for some of the first and most successful attempts at what is known as *biological control*. The principle behind this is to use a suitable live predator to get rid of insects or other creatures which are causing trouble to Man.

The idea of this introduction of predators into an area for dealing with pests appears sound enough at first sight, and indeed has usually proved to be very effective indeed. However, the predator which is introduced can hardly be aware of what food is intended for it and what is forbidden, so that the predator can in time become more of a pest than the pest it was brought in to destroy.

No such problems beset the use of the ladybird in this way, though, and it has been employed very successfully indeed, well before the time of good insecticides. Probably the most successful case occurred in California, where fruit growers and other farmers were sustaining heavy losses as a result of the depredations of aphids and scale insects.

The problem here was largely that the ladybirds in California emerged from hibernation about two months before the main swarms of pests appeared. Food in the fields was therefore limited and there were fewer ladybirds around to go into the attack when they were most needed.

One solution which was tried was to import ladybirds. A cargo of ladybirds was taken to California from New Zealand at the right time, and these were released in the orange groves to deal with a serious plague of scale insects. Following this successful experiment, a further cargo was sent from New Zealand, but this time to Britain, to deal with the scale insects which were damaging the hops.

This second attempt failed, for a reason which had not been suspected. The ladybirds, for reasons known only to themselves, were loath to work more than a few feet above the ground, and decided that the hop vines were too tall for comfort. They therefore deserted the hop fields for the easier prey to be found at less dizzying altitudes on fruit bushes in the vicinity.

However, we can take the story of the Californian ladybirds a bit further. It was realized that if the local beetles could be made to hibernate a little longer, all would be well. But to do this was not as easy as it might have been, because the ladybirds did not hibernate in the areas in which they were needed, and moreover no one knew quite where they did go. Expeditions were sent out to locate the winter quarters of the ladybirds, and they were found, in countless millions, among the pine needles in the forests on the foothills of the Rockies.

They were gathered, literally in sack-loads, and brought down on mules, to be stored in cold-rooms in the State Insectary until the spring. Because it stayed cold, the ladybirds did not wake up until, at the first sign of the pests, they were packed into boxes of thirty thousand or so, and sent out to the farmers.

This worked wonderfully. The ladybirds, newly awakened and two months overdue for breakfast, were released into the middle of a feast, and the pests were effectively controlled, to the benefit of Man and the ladybirds.

But even this big advance in technique brought to light a most unexpected snag. The ladybirds, if they had awakened naturally in their normal winter quarters, would have flown west to reach the farmlands, and this urge to migrate westwards seems to have been a strong instinctive reaction. Consequently, when they were awakened in the farmlands near the coast, some stayed to feed on the aphids, but many others immediately flew westwards—straight out into the Pacific Ocean.

You may like to try a few experiments of your own in connection with ladybirds and aphids. Here are a few ideas.
1. If you can catch a ladybird during the early summer, put it carefully into a test-tube or a small bottle, and plug the end with cotton wool. Then pick a few young leaves from rose bushes or runner bean plants, which have aphids on them, and place these in the tube too. I think you will soon see for yourself the action which I described in this chapter. Remember that the ladybird should be released as soon as possible, and should not be kept shut up for more than an hour or two.
2. Examine the young shoots of rose bushes around midsummer, and see if you can find any ladybird larvae among the aphids. These can also be observed at work in a test-tube, as with the adult ladybirds.

When looking for ladybird larvae, you may well find a rather similar wingless creature feasting on the aphids.

This will be the *aphid-lion*, which is the larva of the lacewing fly—the beautiful golden-eyed fly with large transparent green wings which sometimes settles at night on the glass of a lighted window. A good insect identification book will help you to distinguish the lacewing larva from the ladybird larva.

The way these larvae eat is very different from the method used by adult ladybirds. See if you can observe this difference. Among live aphids, you will sometimes find many white, empty aphid skins. Why do you think this is so?

3. There are a number of quite marked differences between different species of ladybird, apart from the numbers of spots. Try to see these differences with a magnifying glass, and sketch them.

3 · A Look at Lichens

Of all the living things which we may find in a garden, the lichens are some of the strangest. In the first place, few, if any of them, look as if they are alive at all.

Take a look, for example, at the top of an old wall, or a

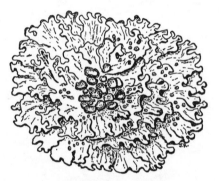

FIG. 3. *Xanthoria parietina*

concrete fence post, or even at the gravestones in a church-yard. Unless you live in a very smoky area, it won't be long before you find patches of orange or yellow on them. And this will almost certainly be *Xanthoria parietina*.

At a casual glance, it looks like nothing more than a

yellowish stain on the stone. It is mottled, wrinkled, and not very interesting. It looks rather as if something had been spilled there, or like an efflorescence from bricks or mortar. At best, it seems as if some plant had lived there once, clinging to the stone, but had died and shrivelled up long ago, leaving just a withered relic of itself.

But take a closer look. If you have a magnifying glass, so much the better.

The patches of yellow vary in size and shape, from about half an inch up to several inches across. The outside edges of them are a mass of yellow fronds or crinkled lobes, standing out from the surface on which the lichen is growing. These fronds are smooth and rounded, but they vary a great deal in size and shape, so that no two are alike. Overlaying these, farther back from the edge, are more fronds, each one subtly different from its neighbour.

Abruptly, towards the centre of the lichen, a change occurs: the yellow mass becomes flat, and here and there are small discs of a deeper orange colour. These discs have a very wide range of pattern and size; some are flat, while others take the form of cups or dishes with orange centres and pale yellow rims.

This, then, is *Xanthoria parietina*, one of the most common of the lichens. The use of the Latin name for it is inevitable, because, as far as I know, it doesn't have a common name. Very few lichens do, probably because few people have ever noticed them enough to make it worth while to name them.

Now, this is just one kind of lichen, and one of the most interesting things about these plants is that there are many kinds, which look very different indeed from one another. They can be so different, in fact, that you would probably not even guess that they belonged to the same family of plants at all.

Take *Parmelia physodes*, for example. You can find this one quite commonly on the branches and twigs of old trees, in the form of greyish-green rosettes up to about an inch across. If you try to pull any of the rosettes off, you will find that they are rather tough and leathery in damp weather, but can get quite hard and brittle when there is a drought.

FIG. 4. *Parmelia physodes*

This lichen is very widespread throughout the country, and you shouldn't have to look too far before you find it. It will grow on fences or wooden buildings as well as on trees, and quite frequently on the stems of heather, too.

In the depths of a wood, of course, *Parmelia physodes* can really grow undisturbed, and sometimes the trees can become so well covered with the lichen that there is hardly any bark to be seen. I have seen one remote wood near Machynlleth, in Montgomeryshire, where this lichen had almost taken over from all the other vegetation. All this takes time, because lichens are some of the slowest-growing plants one can imagine: rosettes which are only three-quarters of an inch across may well have taken five or ten years to get to that size.

Another lichen of the trees is *Usnea florida*: again quite different from the other two I've mentioned. You are much less likely to find this one, as it is not very common, especially where the air is dirty, but it is well worth looking for. At a distance, it looks very much like a ball of green cotton waste, two or three inches in diameter, on the branch of a tree.

FIG. 5. *Usnea florida*

When you look more closely, the balls are rather like tangled wool, but a really close look brings a surprise. *Usnea*, through a small magnifying glass, becomes something straight from the wilder reaches of science fiction: it is weird and unfamiliar, like some creature from another planet, and yet at the same time it is graceful and beautiful in a totally alien way.

But it is not only overhead that one should look for lichens. Some of the most interesting kinds grow on the ground, close around the base of trees, or under scrub and gorse and heather. These often have a very different appearance from the kinds which grow on trees and walls.

Some are in the shape of horns, standing on their points, looking grey-powdered and crusted. Some are like miniature antlers, branching over and over again, smooth, red-brown and glistening. Some have stems which look gnarled and twisted, like the branches of trees in an ancient forest, each one topped with a vivid scarlet cluster of fruits.

FIG. 6. *Cladonia* Lichens
The giants among them are fully half an inch tall

These lichens of the ground are almost too small to be seen from a standing position, and you would certainly overlook them completely while walking. This is a land of dwarfs, where many are so small that a single raindrop would engulf them. The giants among them are fully half an inch tall.

This is just a beginning. The lichens I've mentioned are only a very few of the kinds which you can find. Even within the same species, there seems to be no end to the variety of form which they can adopt. You may be able to pick two daffodils or two tulips which are almost indistinguishable from one another, but individual lichens are as unique as fingerprints.

But what *is* a lichen? So far, I've merely called them plants, and left it at that. This is not strictly true, because a lichen is not *one* plant, but *two* plants in one. It is an example of symbiosis—the living together of two different types of organism.

The two plants concerned in this case are an alga and a fungus, which have developed a remarkable way of living together, so closely that they produce what seems like a new plant altogether, that is, a lichen. So well do they succeed, in fact, that until about two hundred years ago it was thought that lichens were varieties of moss, because no one had any idea of their real nature.

Now, many kinds of algae and fungi live quite separate existences. The green slime of ponds and fish tanks is a collection of millions of algae—soft green, very simple plants, which, like all the more complex green plants, can manufacture their own food from carbon dioxide in the air, water, and traces of salts, by means of chlorophyll, which enables them to use the energy of sunlight to build up the food they need. Algae can look after their own food supplies very well and very simply, but they are vulnerable to drought conditions and to physical damage.

Fungi, on the other hand, don't make their own food. They need to have organic material made for them by other plants or animals before they can feed. Some, like the mushrooms and toadstools, are saprophytes, that is to say they live on dead organic matter such as leaf mould, humus, etc. Others are parasites, and feed on a living host, tapping the food supply which it has produced. The hosts are usually plants, but a few of the fungi are parasitic on animals, and these specialized fungi are responsible for conditions such as athlete's foot, and a number of unpleasant tropical diseases.

In the lichens, the algae and the fungi have got together, in a system of mutual help. The alga produces the food from the air and the rain, not only for itself but for the fungus also. The fungus, for its part, builds up a tough protective covering for the alga.

This turns out to be a wonderfully effective arrangement. The algae are surrounded by a leathery fungal sheath, so that they can grow in places where the rain can fall freely on them, with little danger of damage or of being washed away. In wet weather, the sheath is pliable and allows the water to pass through easily enough to the algae inside. In drought, the sheath hardens, so that the moisture inside is retained. The fungus can live, with the alga to feed it, on bare rock where no food would otherwise be available.

The net result of this system is that both alga and fungus have a far greater chance of survival when living together than they would if they were to fend for themselves. When conditions are good, they can make the most of them; when things get hard they are able to hold out together.

It is because of the success of this symbiosis that lichens are to be found in nearly every area of the world, from the arid conditions of the desert to the tropical rain forests. In the arctic tundra there is a lichen which is called Reindeer Moss; this is one of the few which does have a popular name, if an inaccurate one. Reindeer Moss has tremendous value, as it provides the staple food of reindeer herds when there is no other vegetation around to keep them alive.

The algae appear to have retained much of their independence. The several kinds of alga which form lichens seem to be no different from algae growing on their own. In fact, in all cases of which we know, the algae in a lichen can be separated from the fungus, and they will continue growing on their own, if conditions are suitable.

The fungi of lichens, however, are in a different situation altogether. They have evidently found the symbiotic arrangement so satisfactory that over millions of years they have come to rely on the algae absolutely. Separate the algae from them for very long, and they will die, except under very carefully controlled conditions in the laboratory. They have adapted to the extent that they can no longer make use of food unless it is presented to them in just about the same way that the alga does.

This successful partnership enables the lichens to grow in places and under conditions in which few other living things could survive. They can, for example, stay alive for many months without any moisture at all. They can be dried out and baked in the sun, and yet, when the rain or dew does finally come, they can soften and swell and start to grow again. In many cases, you can break a lichen into small pieces, and each piece will start all over again to produce a new plant.

We do not know for certain yet whether or not there is any life on Mars, which appears in most respects to be a dead and desiccated planet. It seems likely, however, that if any kind of life has persisted there from a perhaps less unfriendly age, it may well be something very much like a lichen.

When we are dealing with plants as strange and variable

as the lichens, we might expect them to reproduce their kind in odd ways. In fact there is no one way of reproduction, and some lichens can employ several methods.

The most common way is strange, in that it shows the one time when the mutual help system seems to break down. Many lichens reproduce by making spores—small dry seed-like bodies, which may be round, long like needles, kidney-shaped, and so on, but only a few thousandths of an inch in size. These are blown about by the wind or washed by the rain, so that they may germinate many miles from the parent lichen.

Now, these spores contain only the fungus part of the lichen. If they are grown in the laboratory, it is only the fungus which we get, with no alga, so that the lichen does not form. Probably what happens in normal circumstances is that some of the spores land on a rock or a tree where a suitable alga is already growing, so that the lichen can be produced once again.

Some lichens seem to have overcome the hazards of this independent way of going about things. They produce *soredia* instead of spores, and these are tiny powdery granules which *do* contain both the components necessary for the growth of new lichens. Although it is not possible to see it without a microscope, each of the soredia is found to consist of a tangle of fungus threads, with a few cells of the alga trapped between them.

There are other ways of reproducing which lichens use as well. Some produce small out-growths from the main body of the lichen, which again contain both fungus and alga. These *isidia*, as they are called, are much larger than the spores or the soredia, sometimes being about half a millimetre long, so that they can be seen with the naked eye.

Isidia are usually very narrow at the point where they join the lichen, broadening out farther away, so that they can be easily broken off. Wind, rain, insects, birds and animals may snap them at this point, and deposit them in a new location to form new plants.

These, then, are the lichens, the little insignificant plants which look as if they had died years ago, and which hardly anyone ever notices. They are worth much more than a cursory glance.

If you would like to have a closer look at lichens yourself, here are a few ideas to start you off:

1. See how many different kinds of lichen you can find in your garden, or within easy reach of your house. The most likely places are the tops of walls, concrete posts and wooden fences, or sometimes on low roofs of sheds. You will almost certainly be surprised at the variety which you can find easily—I can see six different kinds at this moment, merely by looking out of the window in the middle of a town. If you can get permission, remove small sections of lichens with a penknife, and examine them with a magnifying glass.

2. If you can get to any open country or woods, look for lichens on the bark of trees and on the soil at the foot of trees. There are many interesting kinds to be found growing under heather and on heather stems. Are any of these lichens the same as the ones which you found on walls and fences in the town?

3. Lichens will keep their shape and most of their colour

indefinitely, and so you can easily make a very attractive collection of them. Most species which you find will be quite common in the area, but don't damage any which you know to be rare. You can mount lichens very effectively on paper or card, using tweezers, and sticking them in position with a little polystyrene cement (the kind used for making model aircraft). Black paper is especially suitable, and shows up the lichens very well.

4 · *Just Grass*

John James Ingalls was a United States Senator from
Kansas from 1873 until 1891. He was eloquent and, by our
present-day standards rather wordy, but his speeches
showed a remarkable exuberance. In 1872, the *Kansas
Magazine* printed one of these addresses in which he spoke
about—grass. Here is an extract from it:

'Next in importance to the divine profusion of water,
light, and air, those three great physical facts which render
existence possible, may be reckoned the universal benefi-
cence of grass. Exaggerated by tropical heats and vapors to
the gigantic cane congested with its saccharine secretion, or
dwarfed by polar rigors to the fibrous hair of northern
solitudes, embracing between these extremes the maize
with its resolute pennons, the rice plant of southern swamps,
the wheat, rye, barley, oats and other cereals, no less than
the humbler verdure of hill-side, pasture, and prairie in the
temperate zone, grass is the most widely distributed of all
vegetable beings, and is at once the type of our life and the
emblem of our mortality. Lying in the sunshine among the
buttercups and dandelions of May, scarcely higher in in-
telligence than the minute tenants of that mimic wilderness,

43

our earliest recollections are of grass; and when the fitful fever is ended, and the foolish wrangle of the market and forum is closed, grass heals over the scar which our descent into the bosom of the earth has made, and the carpet of the infant becomes the blanket of the dead.'

And that—if not exactly in a nutshell—is what this chapter is about. Just grass. Perhaps we take grass for granted more than any other plant; we all know it, it grows almost everywhere, and that's that.

FIG. 7. Just grass

But that is not that, by a long way.

First of all, let's look at the word itself. From the earliest days of which we have any record, grass seems to have been linked in the minds of men with the very idea of growth. The word *grass* is believed to have been derived from an ancient Aryan root, *ghra*—meaning *to grow*. The Latin word for grass, *gramen*, probably came from this word also. The old English *graes* and the modern English words *grow*, *green* and *grain* are thought to have come from the same old source.

Grass has always been of the utmost importance to Man, even before he began to farm, because it provided him either directly or indirectly with his food. In primitive times, its importance would have been clearly realized by everyone, for without good pastures for grazing animals, Man knew he could not easily have survived. It was a matter of vital concern for all:

'And I will send grass in thy fields for thy cattle that thou mayest eat and be full.' (Deut. 11. 15)

Its importance is no less to us; if grass were to die out on the Earth, so would Man. To quote Ingalls again:

'The primary form of food is grass. Grass feeds the ox: the ox nourishes man: man dies and goes to grass again; and so the tide of life, with everlasting repetition, in continuous circles, moves endlessly on and upward, and in more senses than one, all flesh is grass.'

Grass, of course, includes far more types of vegetation than one might think. There is not just the grass of the lawns and meadows; the same family of plants includes wheat, barley, oats, maize and rice, millet, sorghum, bamboo and sugarcane. And about ten thousand other species, too. It ranges from the smallest plants of the annual meadow grass, which may be no more than an inch high, to the giant bamboo canes, with a height of a hundred feet, achieved in no more than two months.

In all, about a fifth of all the land surface of the Earth is covered by grass. The United States alone has roughly a thousand million acres of grassland, which represents about 60 per cent of the entire country.

Then, of course, there are the vast areas of sand dunes in the world; probably about three thousand two hundred million acres of them, or roughly twice the area of the United States. In these areas again, grass is of the utmost importance to us, for certain kinds, well adapted to the job, provide anchorage by means of their matted roots and wind-breaking action. If it were not for sand grasses, huge areas of moving dunes would rapidly take over and annihilate great tracts of fertile land, even in Britain. If it were not for the other grasses of field and downland doing a similar job on the soil, the entire Earth would quickly become a barren dust bowl.

When we talk about grass, then, we are discussing what is certainly the most important plant for Man, and probably for nearly all land life on this planet. But so far, there seems to be little in what I have said to justify the inclusion of grass in a book about the *hidden* country.

Grass is far from being hidden. It finds some place to grow even in the middle of industrial cities. It is all around us, all the time, summer and winter. But how many people ever stop to look at it closely? Grass is hidden, merely because it is ubiquitous and unnoticed.

Britain, which is well known in the world for the rich greenness of its countryside, contains surprisingly relatively few species of grass. It is, as C. E. Hubbard points out, a land ideally suited to grass. And yet, out of the ten thousand or so different kinds in the world, we have in Britain a mere one hundred and sixty, or thereabouts.

This is probably one of the many results of being an island, and the English Channel has, to some extent at least, hindered the invasion of many of the continental grasses, just as it has hindered other types of invasion by men and by disease.

There is another factor which probably contributed to this small number of species of grass in this country. Britain was at one time linked by a land bridge to the main continent of Europe, and at that time it must have been easy for grass of various kinds to spread. However, the series of ice ages which, thousands of years ago, swept down over the country would have destroyed many of the plants, and rendered much of the land unsuitable for grass for long periods of time. The heavy glaciation and the low temperatures would without doubt have wiped out many species, which subsequently had no suitable chance to re-establish themselves.

The fact that we in Britain seem to have less than our fair share of grass species does not mean that the British grasses are not worth a closer look. There is indeed variety enough to provide very great interest. We may have relatively few kinds, by international standards, but we have some beautiful ones.

Look, for example, at the grasses I have drawn: all these are either fairly common or very common indeed. You would find at least half of those illustrated in almost any garden, and would be able to recognize them if you allowed them to flower. You would find many other kinds too: a quick rough count in my own garden in June has shown up fourteen kinds, and there are sure to be some I missed.

Most people don't think of grass as being a flowering plant at all. The flowers, for the most part, are small and insignificant, and of course green. They are not eye-catching, and are much too common, perhaps, to be worth a second glance. Just grass.

But as a simple experiment, here is something worth trying. At any time during the summer, but preferably in May or June, go out into a garden, a plot of waste ground, or anywhere that grass is allowed to grow without being cut. Pick a bunch of perhaps two or three dozen grasses on which the heads, or panicles as they are called, are well formed and open.

FIG. 8. Grasses of the Lawn and Roadside

Take these home with you, select a dozen or fifteen of the best specimens, including several of each kind you have, and arrange them like flowers in a vase. I think you will be surprised at the variety of shape and form, and at the gracefulness of the grasses.

FIG. 9. One flower of Rough Meadow Grass

When you look carefully at a grass flower, such as that of the rough meadow grass which I have drawn, you will see that it is every bit as much a flower as a tulip or a poppy. There are the petals, called *glumes* in grasses, there are the feathery stigmas or female parts of the flower, and there are the large pendant anthers which carry the pollen.

The flowers are tiny—no more than an eighth to a quarter of an inch long—but complete nevertheless. They are green and inconspicuous for the very good reason that they have no need to be otherwise: grasses rely on the wind to carry the pollen from one flower to another, and therefore they need not be brightly coloured and attractive to insects. For the same reason they require no nectar as an inducement to the insect to push inside.

In May and June, when most of the grasses are in flower, the wind picks up pollen from the lightly poised loaded anthers, which are made in such a way that they shake and vibrate in even a gentle breeze. The pollen is produced in vast quantities, as sufferers from hay-fever are too well aware, and is carried in clouds on the wind to settle on other grass flowers, perhaps miles away.

The flower heads of grasses are held high by long thin stems, which, in spite of their apparent fragility, are capable of standing up to a very considerable amount of buffeting as the wind drives the heavy panicles to and fro. Perhaps you have never stopped to wonder just how these stems can be so strong yet so thin and light.

In the first place, the lightness arises largely from the fact that grass stems are hollow. They consist of long thin-walled tubes which at intervals have a bulge or node. At the nodes, the tube thickens and a partition or septum, as it is called, closes off the hollow space. You can see this construction particularly well if you split a thin bamboo cane.

The surface of a grass stem is covered with a thin skin of very tough material, which does not stretch easily. Inside this skin are packed the cells of the plant, soft envelopes which are swollen with water. These press tightly against each other and against the tough outer skin, which holds them firmly in.

You can picture the result of this system if you imagine

a canvas tube into which partly inflated balloons have been tightly packed. The canvas, which is itself limp, is stiffened and held firmly in shape by the pressure of the balloons, yet it is able to bend easily and to regain its shape immediately the bending stops.

Most plant stems are made on this principle of a tough outer skin with the inner lining of soft cells, and you can see well how it works with the stem of a dandelion. Cut the head from a dandelion stem, and then split the stem along part of its length with a sharp knife like the sections of a banana skin. You will find that very quickly the lengths of stem curl outwards, as the inside cells, with the pressure now off them, can expand, while the outer skin cannot stretch.

In addition to this arrangement of inside cells and outer skin, most plant stems also contain strengthening fibres which run along it. Linen, for example, is made from these fibres from the stems of flax plants. In the case of the grasses, these thin but strong fibres are close to the surface, just under the skin of the stem, and if you look carefully at a grass stem you can see the lines of these fibres. With some grasses, the fibres can be felt as well as seen.

These stem fibres are immensely strong for their weight, and they will also stretch quite well, returning to their original length when the tension is removed. They have two main functions in the stem; in the first place they add considerably to its strength and rigidity, and secondly they serve to protect the tiny tubes which lie close to them, and which carry the sap up to the head of the plant. The fibres prevent these tubes being twisted or bent unduly, which might stop the flow of sap.

Overall, the grass stem is a very effective device for doing an exacting job. No wonder we have copied this pattern in many ways, with our tubular scaffolding and furniture, our reinforced water hoses and our electric power lines.

There are some interesting stories which are concerned with grass, and one in particular is worth including here. Cord grass (*Spartina maritima*) is a tough, wiry grass which grows on mud banks in estuaries, and in salt marshes. Until about the beginning of the nineteenth century, this grass was fairly widely distributed around the shores of southern England and of Wales, and also along the coast of western Europe.

In North America, there was another variety of cord grass, *Spartina alterniflora*, which, although it closely resembled the European kind, was rather larger and heavily built. In 1829, a Dr. Bromfield first noticed plants of this American grass growing in the estuary of the river Itchen, where it flows out into Southampton Water. It was quite obvious what had happened: the seeds of the grass had travelled across the Atlantic ocean with one of the many ships bound for Southampton, and these had found a suitable place to grow close at hand.

Over the next few years, *Spartina alterniflora* spread in and around Southampton Water, out along the shores of the Solent, and west along the Hampshire coast to Lymington. Wherever it met the rather weaker local cord grass *Spartina maritima*, it drove it back and tended to replace it.

Then, in 1870 or thereabouts, something remarkable happened. After about half a century of the two grasses growing in competition, *S. alterniflora* cross-bred with *S. maritima*, and produced seeds of a fertile hybrid. Had the hybrid plant been smaller or weaker than its parents, or less suited to the locality, it would have been crowded out, and that would have been an end of the matter. Instead, it was bigger and tougher, and found the environment highly satisfactory.

Townsend's Cord Grass, or *Spartina townsendii* as it was called, began to thrive. It was first seen near Hythe, again in Southampton Water, in 1870, and established itself firmly in a small area. Progress was remarkably slow, however, and it seemed to find difficulty in spreading. *Spartina townsendii* apparently needed twenty-three years to make the short crossing of a few miles to the Isle of Wight. By the year 1900, thirty years after it was first discovered, it had managed to gain only a few scattered footholds beyond the Solent, as far east as Chichester, and to the great natural harbour of Poole in the west.

Suddenly, it was away, after thirty years of slow struggle. Within the next seven years, Townsend's Cord Grass spread rapidly, sweeping along the coast of Hampshire, Dorset and Sussex, and covering perhaps a hundred square miles of mud flat and salt marsh. At the same time it made the jump across the English Channel, and appeared on the northern shores of France.

Since then, *Spartina townsendii* has gone on spreading. Whereas at first it had difficulty in holding its own against its parents, and in particular *Spartina maritima*, the battle is now almost over. *S. alterniflora* is very rare indeed, and *S. maritima* has been driven back further and further, to a few of the more remote areas of its former territory. To all intents and purposes, cord grass now means *Spartina townsendii*.

In many ways, this crossing of two grasses by accident was a good thing for Man. The new grass is tough and hardy, and has a vigorous matted system of roots and rhizomes which binds the mud and holds it firm against the tides. For this reason, it has been deliberately planted in many new areas all over the world, and is proving very useful as a first step in reclaiming from the sea millions of acres of otherwise useless mud and marsh land.

The story of Townsend's Cord Grass holds another point of interest for us, too. It provides a modern and rapidly moving example of one of the varied ways in which natural selection results in a strengthening of the race and its surer survival. *Spartina* has moved, in a very few years, from having two reasonably successful species, widely separated in the world, to having yet a third, even more successful. In the course of a few thousand years, it seems probable that the new grass will not only have replaced the other two kinds of cord grass which I have mentioned, but will also have taken over large areas which are at present occupied by other kinds of plant altogether. In some places, it may have at least contributed to changing the shape of the coastline over vast distances.

In the United States, several species of *Spartina* are very active in reclaiming mud flats and salt marsh. *Spartina alterniflora*, which was one of the parents of Townsend's Cord Grass, and *Spartina cynosurides* both occur on the east coast, and much of Tidewater, Virginia, was built by them. In the Gulf of St. Lawrence and in Chesapeake Bay, this process is still going on, while on the Pacific coast another species, *Spartina foliosa* is building up dry land out of San Francisco Bay.

You can get considerable pleasure and interest from a study of the grasses which you can find even in a small area. Here are a few suggestions to help you start:

1. Grasses will keep in fairly good condition if they are collected on a dry day, and then pressed between several sheets of newspaper under a pile of books for two or three weeks. They can be mounted on paper or card with a little polystyrene cement or gum, or if preferred they may be fixed in position with a few small pieces of Scotch tape. If you decide to start a collection of grasses, it is best to mark each specimen with the date and place where found, and if possible the name of the species. The time of year when it flowered, and the area where the grass was growing, will help in identification.

2. Start your study of grasses by collecting specimens of all the species you can find in your garden, or on nearby waste ground. Whenever possible, take note of the type of soil on which they are growing—clay, chalky soil, sandy soil, etc. Compare the types of grass which you can find in different places, such as gardens, hedgerows, woods, damp fields and so on.

3. If you go away on holiday, keep your eyes open for new grasses which you haven't seen before. When you find some, try to see why they grow where you have found them, but don't grow near your home.

5 · *Just Grasshoppers*

If you were to come across the following line in a book, it probably would not occur to you at first glance that it had anything at all to do with insects.

$$\text{T v} \frac{\text{v}}{\text{b-v}} \qquad \text{E b b-n v-f} \qquad \text{F v b-g}$$

It certainly looks more like some novel kind of algebra, but in fact it is a colour description of a grasshopper.

There are about twenty-five species of grasshopper in the British Isles, and a large number of species of closely related insects such as crickets, ground hoppers and coneheads. On top of this, the grasshoppers themselves can be very variable in colour even within one species, and a system was therefore devised in 1943 by E. J. Clark, as a kind of shorthand description of the colours of the various parts of a grasshopper's body.

The system used is not really as complicated as it may look from the above example. Here's how it works. First, we have the colours themselves, each one being given a lower-case letter which is the initial of the Latin word for the colour concerned. Thus:

Symbol	English name	Latin name
a	white	albus
b	brown	brunneus
f	yellow	flavus
g	grey	griseus
n	black	niger
p	pink, purple or red	purpureus
s	straw coloured	stamineus
v	green	viridis

Then we have the capital letters which determine the area of the body which we are talking about. These are:

T   Total or overall coloration. This refers to the general appearance of the insect. The first small letter gives the colour of its back; the second describes the sides.

Thus, in the example I have given, $T v \dfrac{v}{b\text{-}v}$ means that the insect has a green back and that the sides are green at the top and green-brown lower down.

E   Forewings. These are divided into three areas, more or less front, middle and back.

F   Hind femora. This is the large part of the hind leg, shaped like a chicken's drumstick. The code shows two colours, for the upper part and the outer side.

C   Head colour.

P   Pronotum. This is the kind of head-and-shoulders plate of the grasshopper.

A   Abdomen.

And that's about all there is to the basic code. When this code system is used, it isn't necessary to write down all the headings each time. Thus, if the insect was green all over the back, sides, head and legs, like the Great Bush Cricket, then T v v gives the complete description. There are some further refinements of the system, which enable one to record the colour of various stripes and other markings, but we need not concern ourselves with them here.

It is mainly the long hot days of summer which we associate with grasshoppers. Their chirping song carries over a considerable distance, and they can be heard in July, August and September in fields, parks, along the roadsides and sometimes in our gardens.

When you hear a grasshopper chirping, it is most likely to be a male. Some of the females cannot make the sound at all, and most of the others only do so on certain relatively rare occasions. The song of a female, when she does sing, is very much like that of the male, but is usually much quieter. A female, on her own, will sometimes sing when she is in a responsive frame of mind towards the males, and then she will usually stop as soon as a male appears.

The males, on the other hand, will chirp a considerable part of the time. Most of them have a variety of song patterns, and these vary according to the situation, but their main song is one of courtship.

Grasshoppers make their chirping sound by a very interesting method. Along the inside of the femur, or drumstick part of their hind legs, is a row of perhaps a hundred tiny pegs. These are so small that they cannot be seen properly without a microscope, and they should not be confused with the row of downward-pointing spikes along the lower edge of the leg.

Now, the grasshopper makes its song by rubbing its hind

legs against its forewings. The wings are tensed and held stiffly, and the row of pegs rubs against the more prominent veins on the wing. This makes the veins and the main part of the wing vibrate very rapidly, so producing the sound.

Nearly all grasshoppers sing in this way, but their very near relatives, the crickets, which have a very similar song, produce it in a different manner. The cricket's right forewing has one vein or rib which has a set of pegs on it, and this is rubbed against the back edge of the left forewing. The cricket's legs do not come into the matter at all.

The fact that grasshoppers use sound for mating calls and for other purposes implies that they can hear well. This is so, but the position of the grasshopper's 'ears', if we may call them that, is rather strange. On the abdomen, in fact. It is possible to see the hearing organ of a grasshopper easily enough, if you look at its side, slightly above and in front of the point where the hind leg joins the body. There you will find a roughly oval cavity, which is usually partly closed by a protective flap. Inside this cavity is the tympanum, or external membrane of the ear. It is necessary to look very carefully, because the cavity is often partly hidden by the edge of the wing.

The grasshoppers which you are probably most likely to come across away from the open country are the Common Green (*Omocestus viridulus*), the Common Field (*Chorthippus brunneus*), and the Meadow Grasshopper (*Chorthippus parallelus*). The Common Green Grasshopper is the smallest of the three and may be up to about three-quarters of an inch long. This one prefers damp places, and is to be found among deep lush grass by the sides of roads, and along paths. As its name suggests, it is usually mainly green in colour, at least across the back, but purplish or brown varieties are found fairly frequently.

The Meadow Grasshopper is the middle-sized of the three, and is very variable in colour, having green, purple and brown varieties. You will find this on open waste ground, provided the area is moist, and in the same general situations as the Common Green. This grasshopper can often fly quite well. While most grasshoppers can make pro-digious leaps of perhaps a hundred times their own length,

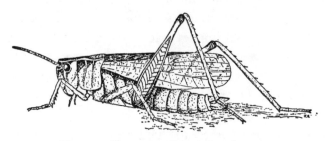

FIG. 10. Common Green Grasshopper

they use their wings only to help in gliding. The Meadow Grasshopper is sometimes able to augment its jumps by true flight, at least for short periods.

Common Field Grasshoppers are most commonly striped or mottled, but sometimes brownish or purple, and very rarely green. They, probably more than the other two kinds, are quite well suited to life in developed areas, be-cause their natural localities are dry and rocky or sandy. For this reason, the Common Field Grasshopper is quite at home on the roadsides, and in areas where there are expanses of concrete, such as airfields and carparks.

Female grasshoppers are generally larger than the males,

and can be distinguished from them by the ovipositor, or egg-laying device, which forms an extension of the abdomen. The Common Green Grasshopper which I have drawn here is a female.

The summer days in this country are few enough for us, but for the grasshopper they represent the bulk of its active life. When late September comes, the grasshoppers begin to die off, and although a few may last through even to the end of November, by Christmas there is not a grasshopper alive anywhere in the country. Throughout the winter, there are only eggs left, to carry on the race next year.

The eggs are laid, up to fourteen at a time, depending on the species of grasshopper, at intervals throughout the summer. They are deposited either at the base of grass plants, or just beneath the soil surface, and then a kind of froth is poured over them. This dries, encasing the eggs in a spongy pod which will then protect them throughout the winter.

Almost as soon as the eggs have been deposited, they start to develop. The embryo grasshopper begins to take shape until it reaches the stage when the pinkish eye-colour starts to show. Then, surprisingly, development stops; the egg goes through a resting period of some months, during which nothing appears to happen. Finally, growth begins again, and, depending largely on the weather, the young grasshopper is ready to emerge at any time from April to June.

The creature which hatches out from the egg looks more like a worm than a grasshopper. It wriggles its way out of the pod and immediately sheds its skin. The worm-like sheath has served its one brief purpose—to help the young grasshopper to emerge—and then it is discarded.

The insect has now become much more like the adult grasshopper, but it is smaller, has shorter antennae and no wings. The nymph, as it is called, begins to eat by sucking plant juices, and after one or two weeks it sheds its skin again. It goes on doing this at intervals, going through four nymph stages (known as *instars*) in all. Each time a nymph moults, the insect which emerges looks more like the final goal, until, any time from four to eight weeks after hatching, the final skin-shedding produces the adult grasshopper.

Grasshoppers cannot grow a new limb if they chance to lose one, but the nymphs can. How good the replacement is will depend on how old the nymph is when the loss occurs, and on how much has been lost. For example, if the nymph is in the first instar when it loses a leg, the replacement will be almost as good as the first one. The second instar would produce one a little smaller than the one which was lost. Later instars tend to grow still smaller limbs, and when the adult grasshopper finally emerges it has lost the power to regenerate limbs at all.

The British grasshoppers feed both as nymphs and as adults on plant juices, whereas the crickets are largely insect-eaters. You can, in fact, keep grasshoppers in captivity very successfully, feeding them on grass, provided this is replaced daily to ensure that it is fresh.

In this country, the grasshopper is merely an interesting insect, but this is not so in other parts of the world. In the United States, grasshoppers are responsible for the loss of crops worth millions of dollars every year. In some states, migratory grasshoppers resemble their cousins the locusts, in their activities, and may completely destroy whole fields of corn, oats and rye as well as cotton, thus not only ruining the crop, but also helping soil erosion. Nebraska, Kansas, North Dakota and Montana are particularly subject to their depredations.

Although grasshoppers are very common, and may be heard chirping during the summer months in almost any place where there is long grass, they are not easy to study. You can, however, frequently catch grasshoppers for examination, by sweeping a large long-handled fishing-net quickly through long grass, especially in June or July.

Grasshoppers are delicate, and must be removed from the net with great care, or they can be examined without removing them. The following points may interest you:

1. Carry out a series of sweeps with the net high up in the grass, and see what you have caught. Then repeat the sweeps, with the net only just above the ground. Do you find a difference in the numbers or kinds of grasshopper at the two heights?

2. In the low-level sweeps, you may catch some small brown creatures which look like grasshoppers at first sight. These will probably be *ground-hoppers*. Can you see how they differ from grasshoppers?

3. Carry out net sweeps in grass in different areas—under trees, in the middle of a playing-field, and so on. Do the species of grasshopper vary over relatively short distances, but in different situations?

In the first part of this book, I have suggested at the end of each chapter experiments which you can carry out for yourself, to find out more about the things which I have described.

I hope that by now I have given you an idea how you can devise simple ways to extend your own observation and study. In the rest of this book, I have not concluded the chapters in this way, but have indicated throughout the text some ideas which you may like to follow up.

As you read, it may be worth while to make a note of any questions which come into your mind, and which you find I have not answered. Then, using my suggestions as a guide, see if you can think out further experiments to carry out. Plan them carefully in advance, and make sure that you are quite clear in your own mind what questions you hope the experiments will answer before you begin work.

6 · The Plant-Hairs

When we talk of hair, we usually think in terms of animal hair. Perhaps, if we have looked closely at insects, especially the moths and some of their caterpillars, we may recognize that these are frequently hairy, too.

In the case of plants, however, hairiness would seem, at first glance, to be the exception rather than the rule. It is true, of course, that there are a few plants, like the garden Lamb's Ear (*Stachys lanata*), which are really furry. Others, like the stinging nettle, can be seen to be covered with bristly hairs, one purpose of which is painfully clear.

Perhaps half the plants you can find in a garden or patch of waste ground are in fact covered with large numbers of hairs, and these can be much more interesting than one might think. Groundsel, buttercup, plantain, dandelion, etc., do not look particularly hairy, yet all have hairs in profusion. You will certainly need a lens to see them properly, and you will have to look carefully, because the greatest number of hairs may well be on the leaves of one plant, the stems of another, the flower buds of another, and so on. You should not reject a plant as being practically hairless until you have made a thorough search. Hairs will be there in thousands, as often as not.

One difficulty with plants is to determine exactly what we mean by a hair. I can illustrate what I mean with a common species of grass, the Wall Barley. This is a grass which you can very frequently find growing, as its name suggests, at the foot of walls along the side of a road, with flower panicles which look very much like cultivated barley heads. Children pick them and throw them like darts, or stick them on their clothes, where they seem to crawl up a sleeve or trouser-leg of their own volition as the limb is moved.

I have drawn one single flower or spikelet of the Wall Barley below. You will see that the awns, or long bristles, which seem hairlike at first glance, are in fact more com-

FIG. 11. Spikelet of Wall Barley

plicated than this when looked at with a magnifying glass. They are, perhaps, not really hairs at all, but long brittle spikes. These spikes seem to carry short bristly hairs along most of their length, but then again when you look closely you find that these also are not really like hairs, but more like thorns, pointing upwards. Lower down on the spikelet are obvious hairs—long, thin and regular, and in considerable numbers.

So you see it is not always easy to distinguish between hairs, awns, bristles, thorns, hooks, and so on. In many cases, it is merely a matter of degree, anyway. A very short, thick hair may be called a bristle; a thick, curved, pointed one is like a small thorn, and may behave in just the same way on the skin.

When you look at plant-hairs through a hand lens, you will find that many of them are just what you might expect. They are long, straight or slightly curved, smooth and tapering to a point. The hairs on dahlia leaves, sweet-pea leaves and stems, the Lamb's Ears mentioned above, and buttercup plants are in this category.

But look now at the hairs on a leaf of aubrietia. At a distance, the leaves look hairless; closer, they can be seen to have a short down on them. If you look as closely as possible, you may just be able to see the individual hairs with the naked eye clearly enough to tell that they are *forked*. A hand lens shows the aubrietia hairs rather like bare trees, or smooth cacti.

Lavender has hairs which are somewhat similar, but the shapes are much more complicated and variable. No two seem quite alike, and there is considerable branching and re-branching, so that the hairs sometimes lie close to the

67

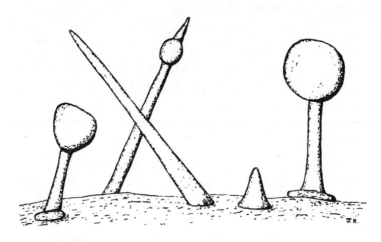

FIG. 12. Honeysuckle Petal Hairs

plant surface and run along it. You will probably find the largest and most interesting hairs on the lavender stems, rather than on the leaves.

At first glance, the chrysanthemum seems to have few hairs, and it is difficult to see the shape of those which are visible. It is best here to pick a leaf carefully and to bend it

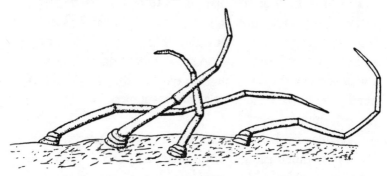

FIG. 13. Goldenrod Hairs

68

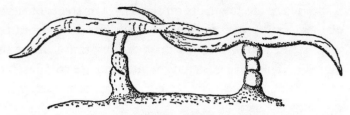

FIG. 14. Chrysanthemum Hairs

in half, so that any hairs where the bend occurs are made to stand up clear of the leaf. This time, the majority of the hairs are T-shaped, the two arms of the T being often wavy and tapering to a point. There are some other plants which have hairs of a similar shape to this, but in some cases they lie close to the leaf surface, and are difficult to see.

For a completely different type of hair, pick a groundsel

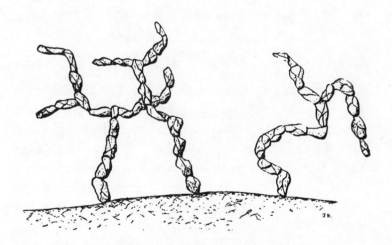

FIG. 15. Dandelion Hairs

69

plant. There are few hairs on the leaves or stems of many of these, but if you pull one of the leaves away from the main stem, you will find a mass of long thin hairs at the junction. These are glistening white, and are composed of numbers of oval cells, joined end to end, terminating in a thin, tapered section.

The sow-thistle, which is a common weed in gardens, has hairs which are something similar to those of the groundsel. However, in this case the cells are almost completely spherical, and strung together very lightly so that

FIG. 16. Marigold Hairs

they seem only just to touch each other. Perhaps because of this apparent fragility, the hairs which they form are twisted repeatedly, sometimes bending at right angles, and sometimes forming loops and knots. You will find these soft white hairs dotted at intervals all over the back of the sow-thistle leaves. In general, the younger the leaves, the more plentiful and complicated are the hairs which they carry.

This is only a small selection from the many varieties of plant-hairs which are easily available for examination: there are plenty of surprises left for anyone who will take the trouble to look. Some others which are worth attention are as follows:

Stinging nettle	Wallflower
Dead nettle	Lobelia
Snapdragon	Plane tree
Hollyhock	Hop
Ivy	Primrose

In many cases the differences between plant-hairs are so great, and the hairs of the species are so distinctive, that it would be possible to make a fairly positive identification of the plant from a tiny fragment of it, provided that fragment carried at least one hair.

7 · The Cultivators

Have you ever wondered how it is that when archaeological finds are made, they are usually well buried underground? The mosaic floor of a Roman villa, the site of a Saxon camp, or whatever it may be, will be at least several feet down beneath the soil.

One reason for this, of course, is that in the course of centuries dust and other debris has settled over the site. But if this were all of the story, the level of the land would now be many feet higher than in the time when those buried buildings stood, and in many cases we know from other evidence that this is not so.

There is a variety of factors which contribute to this burying, but one of the most important is—the earthworm. It is quite certain that without this animal, many of the most interesting and important of archaeological discoveries would never have survived the effects of weather. The earthworms helped to bury them by removing soil from underneath, and depositing it on the surface in the form of worm-casts.

To give some idea of the effectiveness of earthworms in burying objects, it is worth mentioning the work of

Charles Darwin, who was so fascinated by them that after many years of study he wrote a book entirely about them.

Darwin, with the ingenuity and patience which I mentioned before, set up a number of experiments to determine to what extent earthworms did bury things. In one, he covered part of a field with broken chalk and another area with flints. These he left undisturbed for thirty years, to find out what happened. What he discovered was that in that time the worms had buried all the chalk and flints, and when he dug down he found the layers now seven inches below the surface. Seven inches in thirty years—about two feet in a century.

In another trial, Darwin marked off squares on several kinds of land, and counted and weighed the worm-casts on each of these each day for a year. As an example of the results he obtained, one square yielded three and a half pounds of worm-casts per square yard, which amounts to about seven tons of soil per acre per year.

Whatever else you do not find of the creatures and plants mentioned in this book, the earthworm is one which must be available to anyone who has access to a small patch of soil in which he can dig.

We all know that we can find many of these creatures in almost any ground except in desert areas, but it is not generally realized just how many worms there are in a small area. Poorish soils may contain as many as fifty thousand worms to the acre, while good rich pasture land may have up to about three million to the acre, or roughly six hundred in a square yard. A medium-sized back garden, with a rich humus-laden soil, could easily have an earthworm population of a quarter of a million.

Although few people seem to find earthworms really unpleasant or creepy in the way in which many feel about spiders, they are not often considered to be worth a second glance. Worms are felt to be a nuisance in a lawn, which they may spoil with their soil-casts; they may be useful to the small boy as fish bait; they are certainly much appreciated by the thrushes and blackbirds. But that's about all.

In the century before Darwin, the Reverend Gilbert White, who was the curate of Selborne in Hampshire, and a very observant naturalist, had begun to guess at the tremendous value of earthworms. He wrote about them:

'Earthworms though in appearance a small and despicable link in the chain of nature, yet if lost would make a lamentable chasm. Worms seem to be the great promoters of vegetation, which would proceed but lamely without them, by boring, perforating and loosening the soil, and rendering it pervious to the rains and the fibres of plants; by drawing straws and stalks of leaves into it; and most of all by throwing up such infinite numbers of lumps of earth called worm-casts, which is a fine manure for grain and grass.'

Gilbert White had hit on the truth about earthworms— or at least a part of it. In living their lives near the surface or deep in the soil, they do a job of very great value to the world.

They open up and aerate the soil, improving the penetration of water and the drainage of heavy land; they pass the soil through their bodies, changing its texture; they pull down leaves and plant stalks into the ground and bury them; they break up hard soil and make it easier for roots to penetrate.

It may be surprising to learn that there are about twenty-five different kinds of earthworm in this country. Some are red or pink in colour, some yellowish, some grey, blue or green. One is striped, red and yellow, and this, believe it or not, is quite common in manure and compost heaps. It is, in fact, the only earthworm which has a common English name—the Brandling.

If you look carefully at an earthworm, you will see that its body is composed of a large number of ring-shaped segments; depending on the species of worm, there may be anything from seventy-five to two hundred and fifty of these. Although you will find that the worm can change its length and shape over a remarkable range, it is usually fairly sharply pointed at both ends, and the tail is somewhat flattened.

In many species, there is a prominent broad band part way along the body, sometimes as a complete ring and sometimes rather like a saddle. It is often lighter in colour than the rest of the body. This is nearer to the head of the worm than to its tail, and serves a purpose which I shall discuss in a minute. For the moment, it is enough to say that this ring is called the *clitellum*, and is an important characteristic in distinguishing between species. One of the points, for example, which is useful in identification is that the number of segments in front of the clitellum depends on the species of worm, and so does the number of segments occupied by it.

Worms live on humus in the soil, on leaves and other vegetable matter. Many of them live in U-shaped burrows, and at night they can be found part way out of their burrows, feeding on any suitable material within reach. At the first sign of danger, the worm can duck rapidly back into the hole. During the day, it closes the mouth of the burrow by pulling in leaves or stones.

When you go out at night with a torch, you can often see worms half out of the ground in this way, but in order to do so you must move very gently. Worms are blind and deaf, but are incredibly sensitive to vibration, and are able to detect even gentle footfalls. If you do locate a worm burrow at night, it is worth noting its exact position, so that you can examine it again in daylight. You will probably find it, with some difficulty, well plugged and hidden. A tell-tale feature is often a leaf sticking into the ground in an odd way, and standing upright.

Although they are blind, earthworms are readily aware of light, and generally try to avoid it. If, as sometimes happens after heavy rain, their burrows become flooded, they may be forced to emerge, and you can find them in daylight moving over grass or paths.

This kind of excursion above ground is dangerous for the worm, not only because it is very liable to be seen by a bird, but for two other reasons. In the first place, a worm has very little protection against desiccation; it can quickly lose too much water, and weakens, so that it cannot burrow underground again. Secondly, the ultraviolet part of sunlight is very harmful to the worm, and exposure to it for more than a short period will cause it to become paralysed.

Now, what do we know about the way in which earthworms move? To answer this question, we need to consider more closely just how a worm is constructed, because its whole method of movement depends on this.

The worm consists, as I have said, of a large number of

rings or segments. Two sets of muscles are present, one set which runs along the worm, and the other set of circular muscles around the segments. Thus, if the worm contracts the muscles which run lengthways, its body will tend to get shorter; if it contracts the circular muscles, it gets thinner in the area where the contraction has taken place.

Let's see what happens when a worm crawls on a rough surface like a path. First, the worm contracts the circular muscles in the segments at its head end, gradually contracting muscles in more and more segments farther back. This makes the front part of the worm thin. As soon as this contraction of the circular muscles reaches about half-way along the worm, it begins to contract the muscles which run lengthways, again starting at the head and working back.

At the same time, the short bristles or *chaetae* are retracted and thrust out in a similar kind of rhythm, and these help each segment to get a grip on the ground so that it is prevented from moving backwards.

So the worm has a relatively straightforward but very effective way of moving. It thins out the front of its body and at the same time thrusts it forward, the bristles stopping it sliding backwards. As each segment moves forward, the worm lifts it slightly from the ground, to cut down the drag of friction. The whole operation works in a rapid series of waves, which ripple along its body from head to tail.

But this is not quite all the story. It explains well enough how a worm can anchor its segments against slipping, and also how it can pull the body up towards the head. It does not really explain how it can thrust forward its head in the first place, because I have so far said nothing about any pushing mechanism.

If you think about it for a moment, you will realize that muscles don't push; they only pull or release the pull. So how does the worm thrust forward? Coupled with this is the other question—how can it force its way through the ground?

The answer is remarkably simple; a worm has what is called a *hydrostatic skeleton*. All this means is that you can consider a worm as if it were composed of a long wrinkled tube of rubber, completely filled with liquid, but equipped with the muscles I have described.

The skin will not expand unless the circular muscles let it do so; the liquid cannot be compressed. So what happens? If the muscles which run lengthways are contracted, the worm gets shorter, and, because it has still got to contain the same amount of liquid, it must relax the circular muscles and get thicker. When the worm contracts the circular muscles, the opposite occurs; it makes itself thinner, and so it must get longer.

This is where the idea of a liquid skeleton comes in. Muscle contraction can be made to result in a tenseness of the body—a degree of firmness which enables it to push, just as if it possessed a bony skeleton to give it rigidity. In moving on the surface, or in soft ground, then, the worm thrusts forward in just this way, using the two kinds of muscle alternately. If the soil is harder, a slightly different technique is needed. The worm now makes its head end very thin and pointed by hard contraction of the circular muscles, and pushes it forward into a crack or small gap between soil particles.

Having driven it in like a wedge, it relaxes these circular muscles and contracts both kinds of muscles farther back along the body. This has the effect of making the wedge swell, so that it forces the soil apart to produce a tunnel. In some cases, when the going is really difficult, the worm can supplement this method by merely eating its way through, and allowing the unwanted soil to pass through its body.

The earthworm has been using the hydraulic wedge method for forcing its way through soil for hundreds of millions of years. It has just recently been rediscovered by Man as an effective way of splitting rock and concrete without explosives!

If you put an earthworm in a glass tank without a lid, you will very soon find that it can climb up the smooth vertical sides and escape quite easily. It does this largely by means of the mucus or slime which comes from its body, and which allows it to cling to the glass. In addition, however, its mouth is shaped rather like a sucker, and it almost certainly makes use of this to help it to hold on. The leeches, such as the ones which used to be employed by physicians for blood-letting, are close relatives of the earthworms, and they make use of their mouths as holding suckers to a considerable extent.

Worms are very dependent on moisture in the soil in which they live. As I said earlier, their bodies can lose water easily, and they must make sure that they do not dry out. Under good conditions, the burrows of earthworms are generally not very deep, but during periods of drought they will burrow deeper in search of moisture, and may live eight or ten feet below the surface.

They line their burrows with mucus, which holds the

crumbly soil firm and prevents the wall from collapsing. Under conditions of severe drought, many worms can make use of this mucus to line a small chamber, deep underground, in which the worm can curl up and wait for rain. The lining of mucus seals the walls of the chamber, and so helps to prevent it drying out.

In very wet weather, the burrows may sometimes flood, and this is when you will see worms out on the surface. For short periods of several hours, worms can live completely under water if it is well aerated, but they would drown in time if they did not escape.

The digestive system of an earthworm is relatively simple. Food, or soil containing food, is taken in at the mouth and passes through a crop, gizzard and intestine which together run the entire length of the body. You can see much of this system very clearly if you hold a worm up against a strong light, and look through it. It is only some species of worm which come to the surface to deposit the waste material as casts; other kinds line this material out along the walls of their burrows.

Earthworms have a small brain, but the real use it serves is a bit of a problem, because it appears that in many cases the worm can manage quite well without its brain at all. We know that these worms normally have a brain, because this can be found by dissecting them. If a worm loses its brain through an accident, or if it is removed, we find that the worm still continues to live and respond as before, and to be little the worse for the loss. Nevertheless, after a short while it does grow a new brain, so it does appear to be needed for something!

There are various popular beliefs about what happens if

an earthworm is cut in half, as they so often are during gardening. Some will tell you that the two halves will re-join, and that the clitellum or saddle is the scar where this has occurred; others that the head end will live while the tail will die, and some that both head and tail will become complete worms.

Although earthworms do not regenerate lost parts of the body as readily as do some of the aquatic worms, they nevertheless can do this. There is little chance that a cut worm would re-join in nature, although it can be made to happen in the laboratory. However, it is perfectly true that the head end can grow a new tail and the tail end a new head, provided conditions are suitable and the piece is large enough to stay alive for the necessary time. In general, the less that has been lost from either end, the more likely it is that the worm will survive.

In passing, it is worth mentioning that some of the worms which live in water are much better at this than the earthworm. Some even break up spontaneously into quite small pieces as a means of reproduction, each piece growing into a complete new worm.

It would seem unlikely that any creature so low in the scale of animal life would be able to learn. However, it has been shown that a very limited learning power does exist. Worms can be trained to take a particular route, right or left, when they are put into a maze consisting of T- or Y-junctions.

This training can be done by putting something pleasant in, say, the right-hand path, and presenting something un-pleasant, such as a mild electric shock, in the other. It has been found that worms can learn which path to take after a while, and can remember for several days, even after the incentive has been removed.

Again, the real function of the earthworm's brain is puzzling, because it seems to have little or no connection with learning power. A worm which has lost its brain will learn just as easily as one with a brain, and will remember just as well.

But we have still not finished with the surprises and interest from this strange creature. In its breeding it is just as strange as in everything else.

In the first place, earthworms are hermaphrodite, that is to say they are both sexes at once. Any two adult earthworms can form a mating pair, and both will lay fertile eggs.

When two worms mate, they lie closely side by side, head to tail. They are held firmly together, partly by the chaetae or bristles, and partly by bands of mucus. Sperm is interchanged, but instead of going directly to the eggs or into the body of the worm, it is stored just in front of the point where the eggs will emerge.

Shortly after mating, the worm produces a kind of band of protein, like a ring round its body over the saddle or clitellum. When this is ready, and has been filled with a kind of egg-white, the worm begins to wriggle backwards out of this band, moving it towards its head. As it does so, the eggs are laid into the band and are fertilized as the band passes over the point where the sperm have been stored since mating.

When the band containing the fertilized eggs reaches the worm's head, it comes away, the end of the band closing up front and back to form a lemon-shaped egg-case. This dries to form a tough protective cocoon until the young are ready to emerge.

There is much more to tell about the earthworm—very much more—but this will be enough to let you see that they are creatures of considerable interest. I can do no better than to finish this chapter with the words of Charles Darwin, who devoted so much time and effort to their study:

'When we behold a wide turf-covered expanse, we should remember that its smoothness on which so much of its beauty depends, is mainly due to all the inequalities having been levelled by worms.

'It is a marvellous reflection that the whole of the superficial mould over any such area has passed and will again pass every few years through the bodies of worms. The plough is one of the most ancient and valuable of man's inventions; but long before he existed the land was in fact regularly ploughed and still continues to be ploughed by earthworms. It may be doubted whether there are many other animals which have played such an important part in the history of the world as these lowly organized creatures.'

8 · Shadows of the Coal Forest

Five hundred million years ago, the oceans already teemed with life. Worms, sponges, molluscs and so on abounded in the warm shallow seas, and trilobites, which looked very much like living kippers, scuttled over the sand and among the rocks. Nearer the surface, huge jellyfish drifted and fed on the many tiny creatures which inhabited the sunlit water.

Seaweeds, many of them very different from those which we know today, grew in great drifts, and some, having adapted themselves to brackish and fresh water, crowded the estuaries and creeks until the water was trapped and the pools were filled with vegetation.

Above the water, however, it was a very different story. No plant grew on the shores or on the sloping banks of the rivers; the plains and hillsides were barren rock and sand. There were no animals, no insects, no living things.

For more than a hundred million years, the situation on land stayed the same. The climate was hot and wet. Torrential rains lashed the mountains; winds and dust-storms ground them down, and mighty rivers carried away the debris to be deposited in the seas. In many places, volcanoes spewed out millions more tons of carbon dioxide into the atmosphere, and this gas, being very dense, lay close to the ground like a blanket over the Earth. The carbon dioxide allowed the sun's light to pass through, and this light turned into heat when it was absorbed by the rocks and water. A lot of this heat was then trapped, because the gas slowed down the loss of heat into space, so the temperature of the Earth rose still further.

More kinds of life appeared in the seas: scorpion-like creatures with claws like crabs', shell-fish of many varieties, and cephalopods which bore marked similarities to some present-day members of the octopus family. On land, all remained silent and bare.

Then, about three hundred and seventy million years ago, a tremendous change began to take place. Plants, which had previously confined themselves to the water, started to emerge from the pools and shallow inlets, and to grow above the surface, in the wet mud.

At first, the difference which it made to the scene cannot have been very great. The plants kept close to the water, growing with their roots submerged, and rising no more than a few inches above the ground. But this was a beginning.

The next seventy million years saw a remarkable change in the appearance of the land. While the hills and mountains and the great dry plains remained bare, the low-lying ground was transformed. In the area which is now part of Glamorgan and Monmouthshire, for example, great swamps developed; rivers fed in vast quantities of fresh water, and vegetation dammed up the flow to form pools and lakes which now teemed with newer forms of life—

primitive crustaceans, snails and fish. In the deeper rivers and pools, sharks hunted.

The majority of the plants had still not moved far from the water, but some of them had increased tremendously in size. Trees, some more than a hundred feet tall, reared up around the margins of the swamps, and many grew directly out of the water. This was the age of the coal forests.

It must have been a strange and awesomely beautiful sight, one of these swamp-forests. The trees, or at least many of them, would have seemed oddly familiar to us, although they were not like any trees which we now know. Lepidodendrons, for example, grew up straight and tall from the shores of the lakes, their heads bearing clusters of cone-like fruits. At their feet were ferns, some low-lying or creeping over fallen trees; others, while shorter than the lepidodendrons, were nevertheless tree-like, with stocky trunks above which the massive fronds swept and curled out. Still more ferns grew like the lianas of modern tropical forests, winding around the tall trees and climbing high into the sunlight.

On the ground there was no grass, for the grasses had not yet evolved. Instead, the soft mud and moist soil would have been covered thickly with bright green algae and with strange mosses which spread in and out of the shallower pools.

The water stretched out in ponds and lakes between the belts of forest, and other trees—the horsetails—grew out of the mud and from the water itself. These grew thickly in groves, their stiff branch-like arms intertwined and tangled, while they reached up to a height of a hundred feet or more.

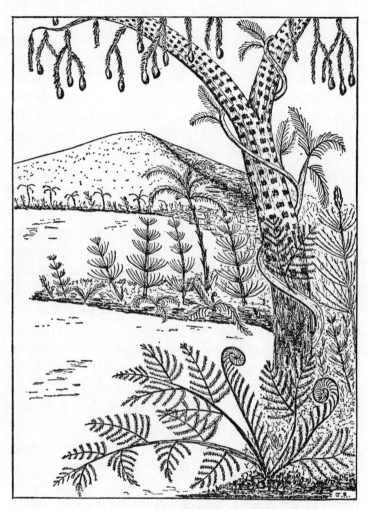

FIG. 17. A Coal-forest Swamp

Water was abundant, the climate was sub-tropical, and trees and other vegetation ran riot. In many parts the forest must have been impenetrably dense, so that the sunlight could barely reach down to the ground or water beneath.

It was a quiet world, in which the main sounds, apart from the wind and rain, would have been made by the old trees crashing down into the swamp. Vegetation dammed the streams and flooded new areas; rivers carrying millions of tons of silt from the plains and mountains were diverted from their courses, and these buried the mosses, ferns and fallen trees under the mud, where, over the millions of years which followed, they became black coal.

Scorpions and spiders hunted in the undergrowth of the coal forests; their prey were insects which somewhat resembled our grasshoppers and cockroaches. They, in turn, would have fallen victim to the lizard-like amphibians, which lived in and around the pools and streams. Overhead, the forerunner of the flying insects soared—*Meganeura*, the dragonfly with wings two to two and a half feet across.

The plants and trees which I have mentioned above belong to a class known as *cryptogams*, or non-flowering plants, which reproduce by means of spores and not by seeds. The ferns, mosses, horsetails, algae, lichens and fungi fall into this category.

The difference between spores and seeds is generally quite a clear-cut one, although there are some exceptions which we need not consider here. Spores are extremely simple—tiny single cells—which are produced by the plant without any fertilization process. Seeds are larger, are produced as the result of sexual fertilization, and are many-celled.

In the seed, a considerable amount of the development of the new plant has already taken place. You can see this very clearly if you soak a bean in water for several hours, carefully strip off the outer skin, and prise open the two halves, or cotyledons. With the naked eye you will be able to see the rudimentary root projecting from the edge and the short stem of the young plant pointing inwards. If you look at the tip of this stem with a lens, the beginnings of the first leaves are just visible.

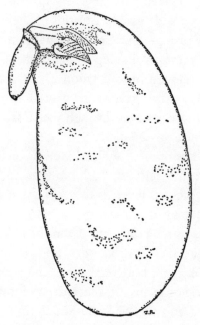

FIG. 18. Runner Bean, showing development in the seed

The seed contains the whole plant in embryo, together with a food supply to start it going. In a spore, none of this embryo plant is there. The spore is merely a cell of the plant, sometimes encased in a tough protective sheath.

The earliest plants of the coal forests, then, employed this simple spore method of reproduction. There were, it is true, one or two attempts on the part of some plants to develop a seed-type method, but for some unknown reason these were not very successful, and the plants which employed them became extinct. It was not until later that the forerunners of the true seed-bearing plants emerged and stayed to take over the world.

Not so with the cryptogams, however. The first cryptogams were all low-lying plants, perhaps rather like our present-day algae and mosses. But out of these developed a new kind of plant—the *vascular* cryptogam. The word vascular merely means 'having vessels', and the vascular cryptogams developed fibrous wood-like structures called vascular bundles, which gave to the plant both rigidity and a series of vessels or passages through which sap could flow to the higher parts of the plant.

It was this development which made the erect tree-like plant possible: the ferns and clubmosses and horsetails emerged and reached upwards towards the sunlight. The first real forests had begun.

Now, all this seems a long way from the hidden country of our gardens, parks and roadsides. So it is, in both time and subject. Yet there is a connection, and a close one.

The giant cryptogams of the ancient forests did not survive for long, in terms of evolutionary time. By the end of the Permian period, about a hundred and fifty million years after they had emerged, they had virtually died out, to be replaced by the host of more complex and more versatile flowering trees.

But at the same time as the giants, there were many more humble cryptogams—ferns, horsetails, clubmosses and so on, of much smaller size. These did not die out. Perhaps because they were smaller, perhaps because they did not become so specialized as the giants, and because they were more able to cope with a changing environment, they survived.

There have been some changes, it is true, but many of the vascular cryptogams which we have today are very similar indeed to those which flourished three hundred million years ago. The clubmosses now grow to a height of a foot or two at the most, and few ferns are now more than several feet tall. Some South American horsetails exist which will form small forests up to twenty feet high, but these are the exception, and horsetails elsewhere are shorter than a man.

They are still here, however. In a sense, they are living fossils, because, by a comparison of the similarities and differences between modern plants and the fossils in the coal beds, we can deduce much more than we otherwise might about the ancient forests and the course which evolution has taken.

And now we must look at several of these plants as they are at present, after several hundred million years of evolution. In many ways they are still remarkably primitive. To begin with, take the ferns. Many of these show very close resemblances to the ferns of the coal forests as we see them in the fossil records. Most of the ferns which you will find in this country are relatively small, although the most common of all—the bracken—can reach a height of over seven feet under suitable conditions.

The Victorian period was a great time for fern-collecting, and houses, gardens and parks were filled with them. Unfortunately this interest did much to reduce the fern population in Britain, and many of the most beautiful species are now rare. If you do find an unusual fern at any time, growing wild, there is a better and more interesting way of obtaining one than digging it up, and I shall describe this in a moment.

The Royal Fern, the largest and one of the most spectacular to grow in this country, suffered badly from the depredations of the fern collectors. You will find it now only in a few of the more or less isolated areas, mainly in the western counties. This is a truly magnificent plant when grown under good conditions, and, having changed relatively little for many millions of years, it gives us a good idea of what some of the smaller tree ferns of the coal forests must have been like.

It has a massive rootstock, which in many ways resembles a short trunk, and which, on a large plant perhaps two or three hundred years old, may weigh several hundred pounds. The plant can grow to a height of eight or ten feet, with huge fronds up to three feet across and twelve feet long.

While you may never come across one of these giants among ferns, except in a large garden or park, you will certainly be able to find a fern of some kind—perhaps the Common Polypody which I have drawn, or at least the Bracken. They are all ferns, and while they differ very much in form and appearance, you can learn a lot about the whole family by studying just one of them.

At some time or other, you must have looked at a fern frond, and turned it over, to see the orange or brown patches on the under side. These are the *sori* or clusters of spore-capsules, and if you shake a really ripe frond gently over a sheet of paper you will find hundreds of tiny spores, just visible to the naked eye, falling on to it.

These clusters of spore-capsules are well worth study with a hand lens. On many ferns they are very beautiful, and vary considerably in appearance as they ripen. In some cases, the spore-capsules (*sporangia*) are not covered; in some there is a fine papery scale over the top of them,

FIG. 19. Common Polypody

which peels back as they ripen. Sporangia are smooth glossy spheres, sometimes pale in colour, sometimes a rich brown. Often they are surrounded by a taut ring which, when the spores are ripe, will break, snapping the two halves of the sporangium apart, and flinging out the spores violently.

This action is not difficult to see, if you can pick carefully a fern frond on which the spores are ripe and on which some can be seen to have already been shed. You can test

93

whether or not the spores are in the right condition by gently shaking the frond over a piece of paper, when spores will fall if it is suitable.

Take the frond into a warm dry atmosphere, preferably in the sun, and watch through the hand lens. In a few minutes you will be able to see sporangia exploding at quite frequent intervals as the final ripening occurs.

It is quite easy to see the development of these spores, if you wish, and at the same time to obtain new fern plants. All you need to do is this. First, get a small quantity of peat, preferably in the form of a compressed block, and scald this with boiling water to kill any seeds or fungi which may be present. Then, when it is cold, place this in a dish or on a plate, so that it is standing in about a quarter of an inch of water with the top of the peat an inch or so above the water. Next, sprinkle the collected spores over the top of the moist peat, and cover the peat with a sheet of glass or an inverted glass pie-dish.

You will have to wait now for anything from several days to a few months, depending on the kind of fern. You will then see a greenish tinge appear in patches on the surface of the peat, where the spores have started to grow.

The minute green patch which develops from each spore is nothing like a fern. If you look at one with a hand lens, you will see that it is flat and probably heart-shaped, with small rootlets going from the under side of it into the peat. This is known as a *prothallus*.

The odd thing about the reproduction of ferns is that it is a two-step process. The spores are produced by a non-sexual process. On germination, the spores grow into the prothalli, which then develop microscopic male and female organs.

The male organ, or *antheridium*, produces a very large number of free-swimming sperms, which are attracted chemically to the *archegonium* or female organ, which contains an egg. This egg is fertilized by one of the sperms, and it is this which can then develop into a small fern plant.

If you watch the growth of the prothalli with a hand lens, you will see how the first minute fern frond emerges from the top of the heart-shaped disc. As the plant grows, the prothallus, which has served its purpose, shrivels away. The small ferns, or sporelings, can now be pricked out into moist sandy peat to allow them to grow.

In passing, the mosses are worth a mention here, although I shall not consider them in detail. They are also cryptogams, but are interesting to compare with the ferns in that they have a rather different way of going about spore formation.

In the mosses, a spore develops into a *protonema*, a green thread-like structure, instead of a prothallus as in the case of the ferns. You can grow spores of mosses in the way I described for ferns, and these threads are then visible with a lens.

Buds form on the protonema, and these grow into the typical finely-leaved plants of the moss. However, the stems, when developed, carry separate male and female organs; fertilization occurs when the swimming male cells reach the female organs, and these later develop into the spore capsules.

These spore capsules are beautiful and interesting to study, as I have tried to show in the drawings, which were made using a hand lens. When they are nearly ripe, the little hood or *calyptra* on the top of the capsule falls off:

there is still a rounded top or lid to the capsule, but eventually this also falls away. Inside, the spores are often held in by a mass of minute teeth, which will change shape depending on atmospheric conditions, and which release the spores when conditions are just right for their growth.

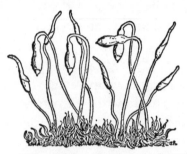

FIG. 20. Greater Matted Thread Moss and Wall Screw Moss growing together on a wall

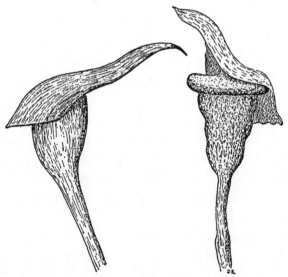

FIG. 21. Spore Capsules of Curly Thatch Moss

I shall not say anything here about the clubmosses, which formed such a significant part of the coal forest vegetation, because these are now relatively rare except in mountain regions, and you are unlikely to find them in or near the larger towns.

Not so with the horsetails, however, which were equally rampant in the coal forests. These, albeit much smaller, are still quite common in most parts of the country, and are particularly plentiful on rough waste ground and on road-sides. If you do find any in your garden, it is a sad reflection on the way in which the garden is maintained, and on the quality of the soil!

Out of the many species of horsetail which existed in carboniferous times, only about twenty now survive, and about a dozen of these occur in this country. Like the ferns, they are vascular cryptogams, but very different from the ferns in appearance. If you are not familiar with these plants, the drawing of young shoots of the Field Horsetail should enable you to identify them readily enough. The older plants have longer branches, and look very much like the tree-horsetails or calamites on the right of the coal forest drawing.

If you can find one of the horsetails, it is interesting to see how the plant is constructed. You will find that the stems are stiff and hollow, with rings of 'teeth' around the stem at intervals. These teeth may be darker coloured than the rest of the stem. When one of the stems is pulled, it will part fairly readily at a joint inside this ring of teeth, so that the whole stem can be seen to be constructed of a series of more or less identical short sections.

The branches of the horsetail are made in exactly the

same way, so that they are like smaller replicas of the main stem. There are no leaves or fronds, and—because the horsetails belong to the cryptogam group—no flowers. So the horsetail is constructed along the simplest lines one can imagine for an erect plant.

FIG. 22.
Young
sterile stems
of Field
Horsetail

The horsetail plants which you will find in the summer and autumn are generally the sterile stems, which are green and branched. The fertile stems, which bear the spores, appear earlier in the spring, and these are pinkish-brown in colour and have no branches. Instead, they carry at the top a kind of cone, which is usually brown. These cones are built out of whorls of mushroom-like structures arranged around the stem, under the caps of which are the sporangia which contain the spores.

If you can find a ripe horsetail cone, it is well worth examining it closely, and also the spores themselves, if these can be shaken out. The spores, which can be seen well enough with a hand lens, are roughly spherical, but unlike the fern spores they each carry two small threads.

When the spores are damp, as in the unripened cone, these threads are wound tightly around it, but as the spore dries, the threads rapidly uncoil. This almost sudden opening of the threads can be seen with a magnifying glass quite well if you first breathe gently on the spores to make the threads coil up, and then watch while they dry out again. The purpose of the threads is similar to that of the thistle-down and the dandelion 'clocks'—they help the spores to ride on the wind and so travel some distance from the parent plant.

In fact, however, although the horsetail spores develop into prothalli very much as do the fern spores, the horsetails do not rely entirely on this method of reproduction. In many cases, because horsetail spores die very easily and rapidly, few new plants are produced by this method; instead, the horsetails spread underground by means of long creeping rhizomes. If you try to dig up a horsetail, you will soon find that what appear to be dozens or hundreds of separate plants are really all joined into one big tangled system.

And so, nearly four hundred million years after they first appeared to form the great primeval forests with which our coal was made, the ferns and horsetails and a few other plants still linger on, having successfully survived almost unchanged while the rest of the plant kingdom became transformed, over and over again.

9 · Slugs and Snails

About a hundred and fifty years ago, an old Wiltshire gardener was asked the question: 'What are snails?' The old man pondered over this for a while, and then replied:

'Well sir, they are not animals, nor yet insects; they are fish, like whelks. They are shell-fish sure enough.'

This observation was not so far from the truth as might appear at first thought, for slugs and snails are molluscs, and the majority of the Mollusca are sea creatures. The Mollusca include three main groups: the Lamellibranchiata or bivalves, which contains the two-shelled creatures like mussels, cockles and oysters, the Cephalopoda, which includes the octopus, squid and nautilus, and the Gastropoda, to which the limpets, slugs, snails, winkles and whelks belong.

One could say that although the various molluscs differ very widely from each other, they have two things in common: a shell and a foot. The truth of this statement is far from obvious, because the octopus and the slug, for example, seem to be without shells, and the Cephalopods in particular appear to have no foot. But things are not what they seem.

The name Cephalopod comes from the Greek words

kephale, a head, and *podos*, a foot, and members of the octopus family have the tentacles, which are really a modified foot, arranged on the head and centred around the mouth.

Gastropod also comes from two Greek words, *podos* as before, and *gaster*, a stomach. The gastropods, then, have one large foot along the whole base of the body, so that in effect they walk on their stomachs. The Lamellibranchs, such as the cockle, also possess a large foot which is used to propel them along. You can easily see a cockle doing this in a bowl of water, if you are patient enough to wait, and quiet enough not to disturb it. In an opened cockle, the orange curved foot can be seen as the most prominent feature.

Now we come to the shell. In most of the molluscs, the shell is obvious enough. The octopus, however, or the squid, does not look as if it has one at all, merely because it is entirely enclosed inside the body. Yet you have almost certainly seen these shells, at some time or other—cuttlefish 'bone', which is given to cage birds for sharpening their beaks.

There is one genus of slug—*Testacella*—which does have a very small shell, very close to the end of the tail, but the others show no sign of one externally. Like the octopus, however, the slug has an internal shell, although in some species this has almost disappeared, and consists of no more than a few grains of chalky material.

There are about 725 species of snail in the United States, and 40 species of slug, although 44 of the snails and 10 of the slugs do not belong to this country, and have been brought in probably by accident. While widespread, they favour moist places because like the worms, they are liable to desiccation, which can prove fatal.

Slugs and snails, then, tend to remain hidden away in sheltered corners, in crevices and under leaves, moss or bark, when conditions are dry, and to come out at night only during or soon after rain, or when the dew is heavy.

FIG. 23. Garden Snail, *Helix aspersa*

Slugs, having little or no shell, and certainly none which offers any protection, are worse off than snails in this respect. They must rely solely on being able to find moist situations in which to lie up when the weather is dry; the snails have other means of coping with the problem.

Helix aspersa, the Garden Snail, for example, will seal over the opening of its shell in dry weather, using a film of mucus which hardens to form a protective door, with only a small hole through which to breathe.

The Roman snail, *Helix pomatia*, makes its door from a chalky material, like plaster, instead of using mucus. This door does not contain a breathing hole, but is porous, so that air can be drawn through it. It is interesting that this particular snail is also called the Apple Snail, because of a misunderstanding over its Latin name. The word *pomatia*, in fact, has nothing to do with apples at all, but comes from the Greek *poma*, meaning pot-lid, which is a fair description of the chalky disc with which this snail closes off its shell opening.

You will sometimes find snails sealed with mucus in dry weather, when they will stay unmoving for many weeks at a time. However, wherever they happen to be, they will know immediately the rain comes, and will emerge in search of food. If you gather up snails which have sealed themselves off in this way, and put them in a box indoors or in a shed, they will open up and try to get out as soon as the weather turns wet, even though no rain can get near them. While it stays dry, they will make no attempt to move or escape.

In some way they appear to be able to detect an increase in the humidity of the air, because a snail can also be induced to emerge by putting it in a gold-fish bowl and scattering a few drops of water near it, even though the weather outside may be very dry.

Although slugs and snails have a bad name because of damage they do to crops and other young plants, only a few of the species native to the United States cause this kind of harm. Most live on dead and decaying material, which is why they are frequently to be found around rubbish piles or compost heaps, and in this respect they perform a useful function. Some will even feed on material like rotting fungi. It is largely the introduced snails and slugs which cause crop damage, and some of these can be as destructive as many insect pests.

Some of the slugs are carnivorous, feeding on worms, other slugs and so on. These are hunters, pursuing worms on the surface of the ground, and down into their burrows if need be.

The shells of snails, as of other molluscs, serve to protect either the whole body or at least the particularly vital parts from attack or damage. Thus, the heart and pulmonary cavity or lung of the snail, together with other organs, are situated up inside the shell, so that they never emerge into a more vulnerable position.

In the carnivorous slug, *Testacella*, which has the small shell at the tail, these organs are grouped under it, although the amount of protection afforded by such a small shell is negligible. The remaining slugs, which have no external shell at all, have a mantle, like a saddle, much farther forward on the body. Under this mantle are the few chalky grains which are all that remains of the shell, and the vital organs are situated below these, in spite of the fact that such a vestigial shell can offer no protection.

In view of the fact that the shell of other molluscs serves a useful purpose in terms of protection, both from predators and from desiccation, it may seem surprising that in the course of evolution the slug should have almost lost it altogether. Evolution does not usually reduce or eliminate useful things.

However, when we look at the distribution of slugs and snails, at least one reason emerges. Snails are largely dependent on chalk to build their shells, and tend, therefore, to be restricted to chalky areas. The slug has an advantage in being free from this restriction. A wider range of country is open to it, and hence its chance of surviving is greater than the snail's.

While Apple Snail is a misnomer for *Helix pomatia*, so really is its other common name, the *Roman* snail. It is called this because the Romans were particularly fond of this snail as food, and piles of empty shells of this species are often found around the sites of Roman camps and dwellings. It was assumed that the Romans introduced *Helix pomatia* into Britain when they came, and of course they may well have brought some with them because they regarded them so highly as a delicacy. But *Helix pomatia* was here millions of years before the Romans, as it is found in the form of fossils from a very much earlier period.

Another argument which has been used to attempt to prove that the Romans introduced the Roman snail into this country is that this species is found only near the sites of Roman camps, and nowhere else. On the surface, this sounds like a convincing argument, until you look more closely into the matter.

Then you find that the area where *Helix pomatia* lives is in the south and south-east corner of Britain, an area of chalk downs, which provides suitable country and climate for this snail. It is also the area where the remains of Roman camps are so prolific that it would be difficult for any snail found there to be very far from some Roman camp or other. Roman camps farther north and west, on the clay soil, do not have *Helix pomatia* around them.

The land snails and slugs have a kind of lung for breathing. In the slugs, this is usually situated under the mantle, and has a direct opening to the air through the mantle, on the right-hand side. This can be seen clearly on my drawing of the common slug *Arion ater*. This particular slug is a large one, up to about fourteen centimetres (five and a half inches) long, and you may well find it in gardens anywhere. It may be brown, black, grey, orange or yellowish in colour, but in spite of this variability you are unlikely to confuse it with any other species, because of its size.

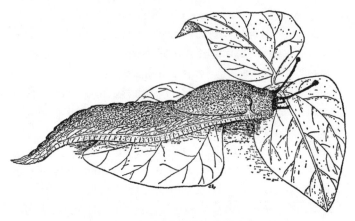

FIG. 24. A Garden Slug, *Arion ater*

There is another slug of similar size, *Limax maximus*, but there is an easy way to tell the difference; if you touch *Arion ater*, it will contract into a remarkably small hemisphere, and will then sway gently from side to side for perhaps half a minute!

The breathing orifice of the snail is situated under the shell, so it is not readily visible. Surprisingly, the same orifice serves for both breathing and excretion; this is probably a means of reducing the ways in which moisture can be lost from the body, as this is a matter of life and death to the snail. One other thing which is of interest about the breathing of slugs and snails is that under certain conditions they can take in oxygen through the whole of their skin surface, and not just through the breathing orifice.

If you hold a snail shell with the opening towards you, and the point of the shell directed upwards, the opening will usually be on the right-hand side. This is known as a *dextral* arrangement, and most species are predominantly dextral. A few have the opening on the left, and are then known as *sinistral*. Very occasionally, you may find a sinistral snail belonging to a normally dextral species, or vice versa.

Both slugs and snails normally have two pairs of tentacles, both of which can be withdrawn into the head if touched. The shorter front tentacles are for detecting scent, and the creatures appear to be able to detect food by means of smell over considerable distances.

The two longer tentacles, higher on the head, carry the eyes. These are used mainly to distinguish between light and shade, and to give warning of any predator coming over them. As eyes for seeing in the normal sense of the word, however, they are poor, and it is probable that a slug or snail can really see at a distance of only about a quarter of an inch.

Like the worms, nearly all the British land snails are hermaphrodites, that is, they are both male and female at the same time. Mating takes place in a somewhat precarious manner, mating snails rearing up on their tails, with the feet pressed closely in contact.

Most snails lay eggs in damp places, and these hatch into young snails which are quite similar to their parents, although the shells are less curled and more transparent. In some species, however, the eggs hatch within the adult snail, and the young are born live.

Twelve to eighteen months seems to be the usual lifetime of slugs and snails, although some slugs have been known to live for three or four years. During the winter they hibernate, in crevices or under dead leaves or tree-trunks, or sometimes in the earth. The snails seal up the shell opening for this period, just as they do in times of drought.

A further interesting feature of these Gastropods is the tongue, or *radula*. The mouth has a kind of horny plate, which is used for cutting off pieces of food, but it is the radula which does most of the work of eating.

It consists of a long thin strip of horn-like material, called *chitin*, which carries a number of projections, or teeth, and these are used for rasping food, as if with a file. Some of the marine gastropods have only a few teeth on the radula, but the land slugs and snails have many, arranged in rows, so that the whole radula has the appearance of a file. In some species there may be as many as twelve to fourteen thousand teeth. The radula is not only used to rub off pieces of food, but it is also retractable, and serves to bring the bits back to the mouth.

Finally, in this short account of slugs and snails, it is worth mentioning their ability to travel considerable distances, and their tendency to come back to the same spot. It is quite easy to carry out an experiment with snails to observe this characteristic, if you can find some which are sheltering, during the daytime, perhaps at the foot of a wall or in some corner of a rockery.

The shells can be marked carefully, with a dab of paint,

or even with a felt-tip pen, so that they can be easily identified again. Then take the snails and put them down in a similar sheltered spot, a hundred yards or so away. Provided they have not fallen prey to thrushes, hedgehogs, and so on, you will probably find them the next day in exactly the same spot from which you took them.

The reason for this return to the same spot is not clear, as it would seem that one reasonably safe spot would be as good as another. However, it seems possible that this instinct may have arisen millions of years ago, at a time when, as in the case of present-day limpets, the shell was adapted to fit snugly the contours of the surface on which the creature rested. The limpet will always return to the same place, although it travels considerable distances in search of food, while under water, and in this case the shell of each individual limpet is made to fit exactly the irregularities of the rock surface so well that it may prove almost impossible to prise it off.

And there we must leave the slugs and snails, to consider a very different creature.

10 · A Gnat called Culex

I began this book with an insect which is no friend of Man—the aphis. I propose to devote this chapter to another insect for whom we have no love at all—the gnat or mosquito. There are many kinds of mosquito in the world, about two thousand species in all, but we are fortunate that in this country there are relatively few.

Of course, not all mosquitoes will attack Man, and the one I have chosen to discuss mainly feeds generally on the blood of birds. It is called *Culex pipiens*. This gnat *will* bite human beings and other animals on occasion, but there is still some degree of disagreement among entomologists whether those which *do* bite us are perhaps a separate sub-species of *Culex pipiens*, which is different from those which feed exclusively from birds.

Much of this controversy arose in the past because of *Culex molestus*, another very similar mosquito, which certainly does bite Man, but which was believed not to exist in this country. However, it does, as was finally discovered in 1934, and it seems likely that *Culex pipiens* has often been blamed for the bites inflicted by its near relation.

Generally, the bites of these gnats are not serious, although in some cases and with certain people they can be extremely painful and cause considerable swelling. Usually, they are merely irritating for a few hours, and the insects are little more than a nuisance which makes some otherwise admirable picnic spots unbearable.

It is a very different matter with the bites of certain other mosquitoes. Some species of *Anopheles*, for example, are the mosquitoes which spread malaria, by carrying the disease from people suffering from malaria, and injecting the parasites into the blood of new victims. This is not just a simple question of passing on a germ as a result of biting an infected and then a non-infected person. The life cycle of the malaria parasite is more complicated, and this particular kind of mosquito is a necessary host for the parasite during part of its life. This is why only certain mosquitoes can transmit the disease, because only they are suitable hosts for the parasites. Yellow fever is spread in a somewhat similar way by *Aedes* mosquitoes.

One of the species of mosquito which can transmit malaria is *Anopheles maculipennis*, which occurs in this country, breeding in marshy ground around estuaries. It is possible, then, to catch malaria in Britain, although fortunately it is very unlikely. To be unlucky enough to be infected, you must be bitten by one of these Anophelines which has already found and bitten a person suffering from the disease, and these are very rare on this side of the Channel.

But to return to *Culex pipiens*. This is a very common member of the mosquito family in the United States, and can be found all over the country. I have chosen it for this reason, because you should be able to find the larvae and pupae of it quite easily, wherever you live.

The adult insect has a slightly hunch-backed appearance when it settles on a surface, but apart from this it holds its body more or less level, parallel with the surface. *Anopheles*, in contrast, will land with its head nearly touching the surface, and its tail end held high in the air.

The male mosquito is a harmless little insect, because it is not equipped with the needle-sharp mandibles with which the female can pierce the skin, and draw blood. You can distinguish between the sexes very easily, as the antennae of the female are apparently smooth, carrying only very short hairs. The male antennae are large and very feathery, as can be seen quite easily with a hand lens, or even with the naked eye.

Culex pipiens females hibernate throughout the winter in holes in trees, in cellars and similar places, where they may sometimes be found if you look very carefully. In the spring they emerge, and in due course the eggs are laid. Throughout all but its adult stage, the gnat lives in water, and the eggs are deposited directly into water, about three hundred or so at a time. They are very tiny, cigar-shaped eggs, which are cemented together side by side in an upright position to form rafts, a fifth to a quarter of an inch across, which float on the surface.

Now *Culex pipiens* will lay its eggs in almost any available patch of fresh still water, and seems to have a particular liking for water-butts or small garden ponds. Even an old bucket half full of water may well be considered suitable for the purpose. It is generally not difficult to find some water where this gnat has laid eggs, but don't expect to find any in ponds which contain fish, for they will not last more than a few minutes in such a location.

The egg rafts are extremely difficult to spot, partly because of their small size, and partly because they are inconspicuous objects which may well drift in to the edge of the water, or become hidden among floating leaves and other debris. However, they are well equipped to survive almost any amount of knocking around and seem to be quite unsinkable. They do not become waterlogged under any reasonable circumstances, and moreover they cannot be capsized, either. This is a very necessary attribute, because the larvae will have to emerge when they are ready through small trapdoors in the base of the eggs, from which they enter the water directly.

The gnat larva, when it is first hatched, is perhaps a sixteenth of an inch long. It already closely resembles the drawing of a fully grown larva which I have shown, but is so tiny that no more than the rough general shape of it can be distinguished with the naked eye. During the course of about three weeks, however, the gnat larva grows rapidly and finally reaches about a quarter of an inch in length.

These gnat larvae spend most of their time hanging from the surface, although they will often allow themselves to sink slowly to the bottom of the shallow pool for a short time, returning to the surface again at frequent intervals with a series of rapid jerky wriggling movements.

Larvae of *Culex pipiens* hang head-downwards from the surface of the water at about the angle I have shown. They do not possess gills or any means of breathing oxygen from the water, so must come up to the surface for air. The long tube rising vertically from the tail end is a breathing tube, which is thrust through the water surface. This tube can be closed when under water, by five minute flaps, but when

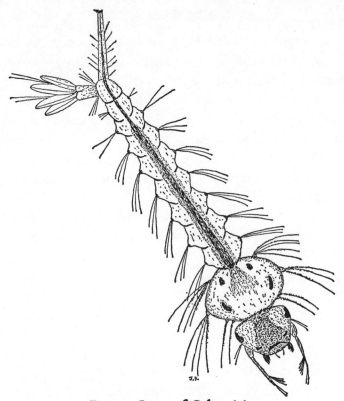

FIG. 25. Larva of *Culex pipiens*

the breathing tube is pushed through the surface they open out to form a kind of funnel.

Just below the point where the breathing tube joins the end segment of the body, there is another 'branch', which terminates in four paddle-like appendages. Although these look rather as if they were designed for swimming with, this is not so, but the exact purpose of them is not known for certain. It is believed that they have something to do with keeping the salt-content of the body constant, but how they do this is not at all clear.

If you look at the head of the larva in the drawing, you

will see two small moustache-like bunches of hair, one on each side of the mouth. The larva uses these to produce currents in the water directed towards its mouth, so that the tiny bits of animal and vegetable matter on which it feeds are brought to it.

The larvae of the *Anopheles* mosquitoes look a little like those of *Culex*, but you can very easily distinguish between them. *Anopheles* larvae do not have the long breathing tube, but the tail segment is itself brought up to the surface. In addition, the larva lies parallel with the surface of the water instead of hanging head down as does *Culex*.

As I said earlier, the gnat larva takes about three weeks or so, depending largely on the temperature, from hatching until it is fully grown. During this time the larva feeds steadily in readiness for the next stage of its life, shedding its skin periodically as it grows.

Then a remarkable change occurs. The skin splits once again, and the long sleek wriggling larva becomes transformed into a creature which bears very little resemblance to it, and which you might easily think was a different species altogether. This is the pupa, which I have also illustrated.

One of the strangest features of this change from larva to pupa is the switch of the breathing tube to the other end. The larva hangs head down from the surface, with the breathing tube at the extreme tail end; the pupa has two trumpet-shaped breathing tubes, at the head end, and hangs up the other way, with its back roughly parallel with the surface, and its tail wrapped tightly in under it. I have drawn the tail uncurled here, in order to show better the general shape of the pupa.

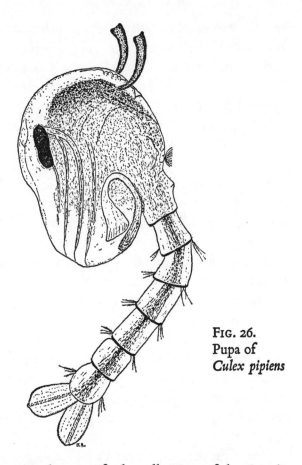

FIG. 26.
Pupa of
Culex pipiens

The gnat pupa does not feed at all. Most of the time it hangs from the surface skin of the water, but if danger threatens it can swim vigorously by means of a series of violent jerks, coiling and uncoiling its tail.

During the pupal stage, the gnat is developing, within the skin, into the perfect winged insect. When the metamorphosis is complete, the skin of the pupa splits all along the back; the insect struggles out, sits on the empty case while its wings swell up to their full size and become dry, and then flies away, leaving the empty pupal shell floating on the surface.

All these stages of development can be seen with little trouble. *Culex pipiens* larvae and pupae will live very successfully in almost any jar or tank, provided they are kept in some of the water in which they were found, and that there is free access for air to get to the surface. The whole cycle of events takes only a few weeks, so that you can see the change in size almost daily.

Because both the larvae and the pupae are reasonably large when fully grown, a hand lens will show most if not all the detail in the drawings, which were made using a low-power microscope. Both larva and pupa make observation under a lens difficult, because of their tendency to dart suddenly away, but you can overcome this quite easily by isolating the one you wish to see in a single droplet of water in a saucer or on a tile. This is not as tricky to do as it sounds. All you need do is to dip out of the jar or tank perhaps a cupful of water containing one of the creatures; allow it to move to the bottom, then pour off some of the water into another container. With luck, you will be able to leave the insect in a small drop of water at the bottom, where it can be picked up carefully with a small water-colour paint brush, and transferred to the droplet for observation. Care is needed not to damage or kill it; it will be much more interesting to look at alive, with the lens.

While mosquito development can be fascinating to study, the adult insects themselves can be a severe nuisance, or even a menace, as in the case of the malarial mosquitoes. It was of course such a study which, in the first instance, provided a method for mosquito control in areas of high infestation. The fact that both larvae and pupae must breathe air at the surface suggested that if a thin film of oil were sprayed on, this would block access to the air. As soon as this was realized, the first real progress was made in the fight against malaria, and vast swamp areas were virtually cleared of the pests.

Even those mosquitoes which do not transmit disease can cause real suffering and difficulty. Look, for example, at the following account, written in the nineteenth century by a traveller, J. K. Lord, who had returned from British Columbia.

'Reader, if you have never been in British Columbia, then, I say, you do not know anything about insect persecution; neither can you form the faintest idea of the terrible suffering foes so seemingly insignificant as the bloodthirsty Horse-fly, the tiny burning fly, and the well-known and hated mosquito, are capable of inflicting.

'A wanderer from my boyhood, I have met with these pests in various parts of our globe—in the country of Cyernomoryi, among the Black Sea Cossacks, on the plains of Troy, upon Mount Olympus, amidst the gorgeous growths of the tropical forest, where beauty and malaria, twin brothers, walk hand-in-hand—away in the deep dismal solitudes of the swamps on the banks of the Mississippi, on the wide grassy tracks of the Western prairies, and on the snow-clad summits of the Rocky Mountains.

'Widely remote and singularly opposite as to climate as are these varied localities, yet, as these pests are there in legions, I imagined that I had endured the maximum of misery they were capable of producing. I was mistaken;

all my experience, all my vaunted knowledge of their numbers, all I had seen and suffered, was as nothing to what I subsequently endured. On the Sumass prairie, and along the banks of the Fraser river, the mosquitoes are, as a Yankee would say, "a caution".

'In the summer, our work, that of cutting the boundary-line, was along the low and comparatively flat land inter-vening between the seaboard and the foot of the Cascade Mountains. Our camp was on the Sumass prairie, and was in reality only an open patch of grassy land, through which wind numerous streams from the mountains, emptying themselves into a large shallow lake, the exit of which is into the Fraser by a short stream, the Sumass river.

'In May and June this prairie is completely covered with water. The Sumass river, from the rapid rise of the Fraser, reverses its course, and flows back into the lake instead of out of it. The lake fills, overflows, and completely floods the lower lands. On the subsidence of the waters, we pitched our tents on the edge of a lovely stream. Wild fowl were in abundance; the streams were alive with fish; the mules and horses revelling in grass knee deep—we were in a second Eden.

'We had enjoyed about a week in this delightful camp, when the mosquitoes began to get rather troublesome. We knew these most unwelcome visitors were to be expected, from Indian information. I must confess I had a vague suspicion that the pests were to be more dreaded than we were willing to believe; for the crafty red-skins had stages erected, or rather fastened to stout poles driven into the bottom of the lake. To these large platforms over the water they all retire on the first appearance of the mosquitoes.

'In about four or five days the increase was something beyond all belief, and really terrible. I can convey no idea of the numbers, except by saying they were in dense clouds; truly, and not figuratively, a thick fog of mosquitoes. Night or day it was just the same; the hum of these bloodthirsty tyrants was incessant. We ate them, drank them, breathed them; nothing but the very thickest leathern clothing was of the slightest use as a protection against their lancets. The trousers had to be tied tightly round the ankle, and the coat-sleeve round the wrist, to prevent their getting in; but if one more crafty than the others found out a needle-hole, or a thin spot, it would have your blood in a second. We lighted huge fires, fumigated the tents, tried every experiment we could think of, but all in vain. They seemed to be quite happy in a smoke that would stifle anything mortal, and, what was worse, they grew thicker every day.

'Human endurance has its limits. A man cannot stand being eaten alive. It was utterly impossible to work; one's whole time was occupied in slapping viciously at face, head and body, stamping, grumbling, and savagely slaughtering hetacombs of mosquitoes. Faces rapidly assumed an irregularity of outline anything but consonant with the strict lines of beauty; each one looked as if he had gone in for a heavy fight, and lost.

'The wretched mules and horses were driven wild, racing about like mad animals, dashing into the water and out again, in among the trees; but, go where they would, their persecutors stuck to them in swarms. The poor dogs sat and howled piteously, and, prompted by a wise instinct to avoid their enemies, dug deep holes in the earth, and, backing in, lay with their heads at the entrance, whining, snapping, and shaking their ears, to prevent the mosquitoes from getting in at them.

'There was no help for it—our camp had to be abandoned. We were completely vanquished and driven away —the work of about a hundred men stopped by tiny flies. Our only chance of escape was to retire into the hills, and return to complete our work late in the autumn, when they disappear.'

11 · Spiders

'Now, pray, lady reader, turn not from the following hastily-arranged notes because they refer to a creature so generally despised by the fair sex as a spider. My object is to show you that in the economy of this humble little being there is much to interest the true lover of nature; furthermore, the subject of my gossip has nothing of a repulsive character about it, being a tiny thing, and not at all ungraceful in appearance.'

So began a magazine article on spiders in 1868, and then proceeded to intrigue and enlighten our great-great-grand-mothers on the nature and habits of the 'despised' creature. Although few people will harm spiders, many dislike them, and for this reason, perhaps, they know very little about them.

Little Miss Muffet, of the nursery rhyme, personifies this dislike or even fear of spiders, and she should have known better, as the daughter of T. Muffet, an entomologist who wrote a book about insects.

You will usually find reference to the spiders in books on insects, although they are not insects themselves. They are treated at the same time, I suppose, largely because they are so closely associated with the insects, both as hunters of them and with regard to the places where they live.

The spiders are, in fact, members of the class of *Arachnida*, the name coming from an unfortunate mythological Greek maiden called Arachne. The story goes that Athene, the daughter of Zeus, was not only a formidable warrior goddess, but was skilled in handicrafts of all kinds, and in particular in spinning and weaving.

She was extremely proud of her abilities, and was determined at all costs to maintain her position of supremacy. One day, Arachne, a mortal girl from Lydia, challenged the goddess to a contest, and as Arachne was known to be a very skilled weaver, Athene was reluctant to take up the challenge.

She disguised herself as an old woman, and pleaded with the girl to retract her rash words. But Arachne remained adamant, and Athene was compelled to agree to the contest. The girl selected the loves of the gods as a subject, and began to weave.

Try as she would, Athene could find no fault in the results of Arachne's weaving, and enraged, she destroyed the girl's work. Arachne, in despair, tried to hang herself, and Athene then partly relented. She turned the rope into a web, and Arachne into a spider, and decreed that she should spin for ever, drawing the thread from her own body.

There are nearly six hundred species of spider in the British Isles, and of these there is a surprisingly large number which you might find in almost any area of garden or park. But I am not going to attempt to write about spiders in general, or even to give an indication of the many kinds which you may find. Instead, I shall consider two only—the ones which are commonly known as the Garden Spider and the House Spider.

Now, these names could cover a variety of spiders; in the garden you might find several kinds of wolf spider, which hunt their prey by running, zebra spiders which run on window panes, and jump on to flies, and so on. The one which I propose to look at here, however, is the one which builds most of the large spiral webs which appear overnight on bushes and fences and across gateways. This is the Diadem Spider, *Araneus diadematus.*

The Diadem, which I have illustrated on its web, is a brown spider which is easily recognized by the large white cross on its abdomen, and you should have little difficulty in locating one, and identifying it. It was this cross, quite prominently displayed, which afforded the Diadem Spider a considerable amount of protection in the Middle Ages, because of its religious associations.

As with most spiders, the females are considerably bigger than the males. If, during the autumn when they are fully adult, you find one which is ten or twelve millimetres (nearly half an inch) long over the head and body, it will certainly be a female, the males being about five to eight millimetres long.

I have shown the garden spider in the centre of its web, but you will rarely find one there during the daytime. This would be a dangerous situation for the spider when birds are about, and it would be unlikely to stay there for long. Instead, it spends the day in a lair by the side of the web, coming out to the centre only in the evening, and staying there for the night, unless otherwise engaged.

The orb-webs, as they are called, from their circular

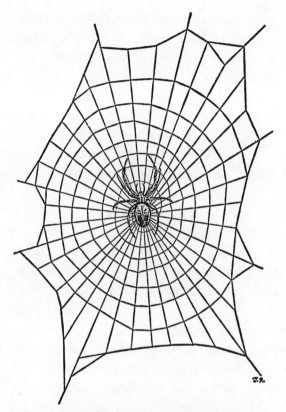

FIG. 27. Diadem Spider, *Araneus diadematus*

shape, are masterpieces of construction, and yet are relatively short-lived. They are usually built in the late evening, and may in some cases be virtually demolished and rebuilt each night. The webs vary considerably in size, and the one which I have drawn, for the sake of convenience, is one of the smallest.

The spider constructs these webs using two different kinds of silk, which it produces from spinnerets at the end of the abdomen. A more or less horizontal thread is needed as a start for the web, and the spider produces this in one of several ways, depending on the circumstances.

If the wind direction is right, it may be enough to stand on one point and to put out a long thread into the wind, so that this eventually becomes fouled on a twig or other projection on the far side of the chosen gap. The spider can walk across this thread, anchor the other end firmly, and then reinforce the thread with one or more additional strands.

In other cases, as for example when the web is to be made across a window frame, it may be possible for the spider to walk from one point to the other, trailing a line as it goes, which can subsequently be tightened as necessary. Yet again, it will sometimes drop on a thread to the bottom of the window, and then walk up to the required spot, taking the thread with it.

Once this starting line is established, the rest of the outer frame of the web is built in much the same way, until the size and basic outline has been settled. A couple of radii can now be dropped from points along the top thread, and when these are crossed over, they locate the point which is to be the centre of the web.

The rest of the radii are now laid in, so that when finished they are all at very nearly the same angle to their neighbours. The spider does this by walking along one thread as it spins the adjacent one, and it appears to be able to determine the appropriate distance at which to keep it with considerable accuracy. This is quite surprising, because as the web does not have a circular outline, the radii cannot be evenly spaced along the outer threads.

Once the radii are in position, the spider constructs a flat non-sticky platform at the centre of the web, and then uses this same kind of silk to lay down a spiral, starting from the centre and working outwards until it comes to the outer frame.

This thread serves only as a form of scaffolding, to establish finally how the spiral will go, and to secure the radial threads firmly at the correct distances apart, ready for the next stage. In this last step, the sticky spiral will be placed in position.

Starting at the outer end of the scaffolding spiral, the spider begins to work inwards, spinning a new sticky thread, anchoring this firmly to the radii, and destroying the temporary thread as it goes. The real purpose of the temporary spiral now becomes apparent. The sticky thread, when it first comes from the spinnerets, is smooth, and the spider tenses and relaxes it repeatedly as it is laid down. In doing this, it breaks up the gummy material on the silk from a continuous film into strings of small droplets at intervals along the silk thread. Had the spider not first fixed the radial threads firmly in the required position with the temporary spiral thread, this stretching and relaxing would pull them badly out of line.

During the daytime, you may find a Diadem Spider in a suitable crack or corner adjacent to the web, or perhaps in a small tube which it has constructed for itself from silk. At dusk it emerges. The web is inspected carefully all over, and minor damage to it will often be repaired. Not infrequently you can find webs which show signs of such repairs, and these are usually easy to recognize, because the mending is not carried out quite as carefully as the original web-building. This happens because the web-building is the result of a series of instinctive actions, each one of which triggers off the next in the spider. Thus the whole process is carried through more or less mechanically. When repairs are necessary, a certain amount of improvisation is needed, and the instinct is less effective. If the web is badly damaged, the whole spiral may be removed and replaced.

These web-building spiders have eight eyes, yet in spite of this their sight is not good. Unlike the spiders which hunt and catch their prey by watching for them or by chasing, they do not need to see well; what is much more important for them is their ability to interpret the meaning of the various tensions in the threads of their webs.

This they can do with considerable skill. The Diadem Spider is guided to an insect which becomes caught in the web almost entirely by the vibrations of the web threads, and it can on occasions be induced to attack even a blade of grass, or a feather, if it is moved in the web in the right way.

Nearly all spiders are solitary creatures, and the Diadem Spider is no exception. For this reason, coupled with the fact that they are short-sighted, and that the females are much larger than the males, mating can be an extremely hazardous business—for the males.

In some of the other species, coloured markings, together with a courtship display dance, play a prominent part, but there is little point in these if one's girl-friend is strongly myopic. The male Diadem Spider, then, must adopt a different technique altogether.

He probably detects the presence of a female by some chemical means, either directly from her as a form of scent, or from the web which she has built. However this may be, he approaches the web with caution, and plucks gently at the threads. He must do this in such a way as to make it clear to the female beyond any doubt that he is a male spider, and not some other edible creature.

Slowly and with great care, the male approaches the female. If his advances should be rejected, he must be ready to run for his life, for a female spider has only two uses for a male. If accepted, he comes closer, but still with great caution, and begins to stroke her.

No other creatures mate in the way in which spiders do. The male, having made a small pad of silk threads, deposits on it a drop of sperm, and then transfers this to its 'pedipalps'—the short furry feelers which can be seen quite prominently on either side of the mouth. At mating, the sperm is inserted into the female by means of one or both of these palps.

The female spider's mind can be diverted from the subject of food for only so long, and it is believed that the stroking by the male actually serves in some way to alleviate the hunger urge. Once this stops and mating is over, the male must escape very rapidly indeed, and in practice many fail to move quickly enough. This may be hard on the individual, but as far as the race is concerned he has served his purpose. The danger is so great that in some other species the males have learned to tie down the females with silk threads before mating, in order to overcome this difficulty. In other cases, mating occurs only with females which are not yet fully grown, so that the male is not faced with so large an adversary.

The young spiders of this and other species employ a

very interesting way of moving to new territory—a method which has been called 'ballooning'. During the late summer and early autumn, the tiny spiders make their way to the top of fences, grass stems or bushes, trailing threads of silk behind them, so that in many cases the gossamer will lie thickly, to be picked out clearly by the next night's dew.

When they reach the top of whatever they are climbing, the young spiders turn into the wind, and begin to spin out a long silk thread. The spider stands as high as possible on its legs, head downwards, so that its spinnerets and the thread which trails from them are raised into the breeze.

While it does this, the young spider holds on firmly, spinning out more and more thread into the wind, until the pull is strong enough. Then it lets go, and sails up into the air, to be carried perhaps only a few yards, perhaps many miles before it again touches down.

So much, then, for the Garden Spider. You can learn much more, of course, by watching these creatures, but you will have to do so wherever they happen to be. It is difficult to induce the Garden Spider to build webs in captivity, mainly because of the large amount of space which they require. If you should wish to attempt the experiment, however, remember that they will feed on live insects only, and that, in common with other outdoor spiders, they require a supply of water.

The House Spider is very much easier to keep in captivity, and I shall say how this can be done in a moment. Although a number of kinds of spider may come into the house from time to time, it is the genus *Tegenaria* which you are most likely to find. *Tegenaria domestica* is quite small, as house spiders go, being of similar size to the

Diadem Spider. The really big ones are *Tegenaria parietina*, which has a reddish line down the middle of the abdomen, and *Tegenaria atrica*, which I have drawn here.

Tegenaria atrica is the big, dark, long-legged spider which comes rushing across the bedroom floor when you have just stepped out of your slippers. The males and females are of similar size in this case, with bodies up to about twenty

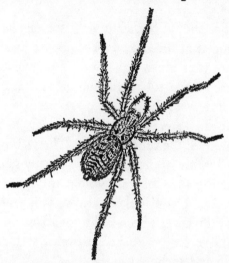

FIG. 28. House Spider, *Tegenaria atrica*

millimetres (about three-quarters of an inch) long, so that they may measure up to about three inches across the legs. They have eight eyes, which are arranged in three rows, but, like the Diadem Spider, their sight is not very good, and they rely much more on vibration, to which they are very sensitive.

The cobwebs which the house spiders produce usually appear to be rather untidy constructions, and do not look like very effective traps for insects. This is deceptive, and in fact, the house spider's web is built very carefully, as you will soon see if you keep one and study its behaviour.

Michael Tweedie, in his fascinating book *Pleasure from Insects*, recommends an excellent way to keep a house spider as a pet in order to observe it. All that is needed is a transparent plastic food box with a lid and a small tube of paper glued into one corner of it, to serve as a lair. And, of course, a spider.

The spider should be left quietly for one or two days after putting it in the box, to settle down and to make a web, before it is given any food. You will find that it readily accepts the tube as a home, and retires to this throughout most of the day.

At night, however, it constructs its web, and may also line the inside of the tube with silk. The web is very fine, and in the absence of the dust which usually settles on it in the open and makes cobwebs visible, it is quite difficult to see. However, if you look carefully, you will see that a network of threads has been laid right across the bottom of the box, suspended perhaps a quarter of an inch above it, pulled tight and anchored to the sides.

These threads of silk will be drawn together at the mouth of the tube, sometimes into a kind of raised platform, and will extend inside the tube to where the spider waits at the far end.

The spider is fed by introducing a live fly into the box—a tricky operation. As soon as the fly touches any part of the web, the spider will come forward to the platform at the entrance of the tube, and there it will wait.

It may be possible for the fly to touch the web lightly without becoming trapped, in which case the spider waits unmoving. However, the instant the insect sticks to the web, the spider will run to it so quickly that it may be difficult to follow the movement with your eye.

A small fly will be seized and carried back to the tube without a moment's pause. If the fly is bigger, the spider attacks from above, so that it stands over the fly, and injects it with poison which very rapidly stops its struggles. Only then is it carried back to the tube.

A spider does not eat in the normal sense of the word. It injects into the body of its victim a digestive fluid which very effectively liquefies all the edible parts. It then sucks out the fluid, at the same time kneading the insect and pressing it, until all that is left is a dry round pellet.

You will find that, a few hours after the spider has captured a fly, this pellet, together with the wings, will be removed from the tube, and carried some distance away, to the far side of the box. The spider appears to choose a 'dustbin' area, and to deposit all remains in more or less the same place.

I said just now that the house spider locates the fly instantly and accurately by the tensions and vibrations of the silk threads. Sight seems to come into it hardly at all, and a spider will find a trapped insect just as quickly and easily in darkness as in daylight. Thus, a spider is drawn to a fly only while the fly is moving, and if the fly ceases to move while the spider is on its way, the spider will stop, and sometimes retreat to its lair without going near the fly.

On one occasion, I saw a fly land on the web close to several dried pellets in the 'dustbin' area. When the spider was within perhaps half an inch of the insect, the fly became completely still, but its previous movements had started one of the pellets vibrating. The spider immediately swung away from the fly and pounced on the pellet, which was about two inches farther on. It then realized its mistake and turned back to the fly, which had resumed its struggles.

For its size, the house spider is immensely strong. It can tackle and subdue insects which are as big as itself, and can carry them swiftly and with no apparent difficulty. This is not restricted to insects, either, for the house spider will deal equally effectively with a wood-louse, and even a young house spider not fully grown will overcome and carry off a large Diadem Spider, bigger than itself.

The house spiders, as the name suggests, are most commonly found in houses, sheds, cellars, and so on. But this cannot be their natural habitat, so where would they live otherwise, and why do they prefer to live in buildings?

The answer is a simple one. *Tegenaria* lives, in the absence of buildings, in small holes or caves in rocks and between stones. You will find it sometimes inhabiting rockeries and holes in old walls—anywhere, in fact, where it can find warmth, security from birds and other predators, shade, and an abundance of food at hand. Its webs, being low-hung sheets rather than the orb-webs of the garden spiders, can be laid horizontally in front of such retreats. When Man began to build houses, *Tegenaria* soon found that these offered all these things, and so he moved in too.

Spiders feature quite widely in folklore in many countries, and they have also played a part in a number of old and trusted cures for various ailments. As these generally consisted in swallowing a spider alive, one might feel that the patient would have to be very ill indeed before resorting to this treatment.

However, this kind of reaction is not universal. We read the following in *Kirby's Introduction to Entomology*, published in the early nineteenth century:

'Reaumur tells us of a young lady, who when she walked in her grounds never saw a spider that she did not take and crack on the spot. Another female, the celebrated Anna Maria Schurman, used to eat them like nuts, which she affirmed they much resembled in taste, excusing her propensity by saying that she was born under the sign of Scorpio.

'If you wish for the authority of the learned, Lalande, the celebrated French astronomer, was, as Latreille witnessed, equally fond of these delicacies. And lastly, if not content with taking them seriatim, you should feel desirous of eating them by handfuls, you may shelter yourself under the authority of the German immortalized by Koesel, who used to spread them upon his bread like butter, observing that he found them very useful "um sich auszulaxiren".'

It is perhaps appropriate to conclude this chapter with the closing remarks of the author whom I quoted at the beginning:

'Possibly, you do not feel encouraged to observe this creature's habits more closely. Do not, however, despise it because it presents few features attractive to the eye. Remember that it is not savage because of its formidable appearance and solitary habits: how frequently are rich colours and symmetry of form combined with seemingly savage propensities. Nor is the gloomy monster destitute of beauty, if by the term we mean simply pleasing to the eye.

Examine by aid of the microscope the several organs of the body—how beautiful their structure, and how nicely adapted to fulfil the various purposes for which they were designed. The disposition of the various parts displays the same consummate skill exhibited in the arrangement of the scales on the wing of the richly painted butterfly, the feathers of the gorgeous humming-bird, or the tinted petals of the flower; and he is no true naturalist who fails to perceive beauty in even the most despised creatures.'

This, then, is what *The Hidden Country* is all about. You probably feel that I have missed out many things which I should have discussed, but whatever I had decided to include in a small book I would have omitted a lot that someone, somewhere, would think was too interesting to be omitted.

But this only highlights the fascination of the hidden country which I have tried to discover: you could go on studying it for the rest of your life, and still find new creatures, new plants, new phenomena, which you did not suspect to exist. I have merely made a selection, and have used my prerogative of choosing what *I* think is particularly interesting and easy to find. What else could I do?

Further Reading

Here is a short list of books which are readily available, and which you would find interesting and useful.

General Natural History Books
The following books are excellent for reference on a wide variety of animals, insects, birds, reptiles and plants. They are also very helpful in identification.

1. A. B. Comstock, *Handbook of Nature Study*, Comstock Publishing Associates, Cornell University Press, New York.
2. W. Hellcourt, *The New Fieldbook of Nature Activities and Hobbies*, G. B. Putnams' Sons, New York.
3. Laurence P. Pringle, Editor, *Discovering the Outdoors: A Nature and Science Guide to Investigating Life in Fields, Forests, and Ponds*, The Natural History Press, New York.

Where to read further about subjects in this book
1. LICHENS
   (i) Mason Hale, *How to Know the Lichens*, Wm. C. Brown Co., Publishers, Iowa.

Like other books in the 'How to Know' series, this is a well-illustrated key for identifying specimens of the subject covered.

2. GRASS

   (i) Agnes Chase, *First Book of Grasses*, Smithsonian Institution, Washington, D.C.

   A fine book for the study and identification of all the grasses.

   (ii) R. W. Pohl, *How to Know the Grasses*, Wm. C. Brown Co., Publishers, Iowa.

   An illustrated key for the identification of the more common species.

3. GRASSHOPPERS

   (i) Jacques R. Helfer, *How to Know the Grasshoppers*, Wm. C. Brown Co., Publishers, Iowa.

   Well illustrated and informative. Good as a reference book and for identification of species.

4. EARTHWORMS

   (i) Charles Darwin, *Darwin on Humus and the Earthworm*, Faber and Faber, London.

   A model of meticulous observation and of carefully planned experiment, giving a large amount of information on the earthworms.

   (ii) R. P. Dales, *Annelids*, Hutchinson, London.

   A fairly technical book, but one which is well written and suitable for older readers. It contains much very interesting and up-to-date information on worms of many kinds, including earthworms.

5. MOSSES

   (i) H. S. Conard, *How to Know the Mosses and Liverworts*, Wm. C. Brown Co., Publishers, Iowa.

An illustrated key. Excellent for identification of species and for general information.

6. FERNS AND HORSETAILS
   (i) B. Cobb, *A Field Guide to the Ferns of Northeastern and Central North America and their Related Families*, Houghton Mifflin Company, Boston.
   Many fine drawings.

7. SLUGS AND SNAILS
   For further information on slugs and snails, you should see the books in the general list I have given above. In addition, the following book is useful:
   (i) J. B. Burch, *How to Know the Eastern Land Snails*, Wm. C. Brown Co., Publishers, Iowa.
   An illustrated key for the identification of species.

8. GNATS AND SPIDERS
   (i) J. H. Comstock, *The Spider Book*, Comstock Publishing Associates, Cornell University Press, New York.
   This is a classic reference book, filled with information and many fine illustrations.

   (ii) B. J. and E. Kaston, *How to Know the Spiders*, Wm. C. Brown Co., Publishers, Iowa.
   Very informative, and excellent for identification of species.

Other books of considerable interest mentioned in this book
1. Michael Tweedie, *Pleasure from Insects*, David & Charles, Newton Abbot.
   A fascinating book for any age.

2. Charles Darwin, *The Origin of Species*.
   An old but well-known classic, in which Darwin puts forward his theory of evolution. For the older reader.
3. Maurice Maeterlinck, *The Life of the Ant*, Allen & Unwin, London.
   An intriguing and informative book, which is easy to read and beautifully written. For any age.
4. Gilbert White, *The Natural History of Selborne*, Everyman's Library, Dent, London.
   Although this book was first published in 1789, some of Gilbert White's descriptions of birds and animals have never been bettered. This is a delightful book, and a model of careful observation and deduction. Rather difficult for younger readers.

Index